PhD Professor Marius Bacescu
Professor of Economics at the most famous universities in Romania (Academy of Economic Studies, Banking Institute, Polytechnic University of Bucharest, etc.). Fulfils the following academic positions: Chairman of the Socio-Economic Cybernetics, Romanian Academy and Head of the Department of Economics, Law and Sociology, Academy of Scientists in Romania. It is the most prolific author of books and articles on economic issues in Romania. Specialized training in the UK.

Daniil Dragos
Engineer in oil rigs manufacturing in Ploiesti. Worked for Control Data Corporation - USA, in Research and Development and later as Market Development Manager for East Europe (computer sales and the first postwar American manufacturing joint venture in Eastern Europe). In Research and Development in Automation and computers in Bucharest. Counselor and Deputy Director in the Ministry of Foreign Trade - Bucharest (negotiations of Cernavoda Nuclear Power Plant, cars manufacturing with Renault and Citroen - France etc.). Fulbright Visiting Scholar at Graduate School of Management, University of California, Los Angeles (UCLA).

Photo on front cover: The largest palace in the world built in Ceausescu's time.

PhD Prof. Marius Bacescu
Daniil Dragos

The End of History as Such and Neoliberalism Forever?!

and Case Study:
Romania After 22 Years of Neoliberalism

Translated from the Romanian by the authors

DEDICATION

We dedicate this essay to all people who suffer from hunger. We hope the decisions makers will think of them as well; not just to their own interests.

CONTENTS

Motto:

"Do not store up for yourselves treasures on earth..."
The New Testament, Matthew 6: 19.

'Then Jesus said to his disciples, "I tell you the truth, it is hard for a rich man to enter the kingdom of heaven. Again I tell you, it is easier for a camel to go through the eye of a needle than for a rich man to enter the kingdom of God." The New Testament, Matthew 19: 23 - 24.

The End of History as Such and Neoliberalism Forever?!

A - *Neoliberalism versus communism*

The Manifesto of the Communist Party - published by Marx and Engels in February 1848, starts with the following words: "A spectre is haunting Europe - the spectre of communism". Between the years of 1989 - 1992, when almost nobody expected it, the communism collapsed in Eastern Europe. The Soviet Union was dissolved in 1991. The lengthy Cold War ended. Not just in Europe, but all over the world, the neoliberalism (characterized by private enterprises, relatively open markets, globalization etc) rules today, triumphantly. The neoliberalism became a fashion and resort to making use of it, not only the political parties that have the word liberal in their name, but also the social democratic and socialist parties. Some of the neoliberal solutions were applied even in China, where the Chinese Communist Party rules the country for over 60 years. Individualism, private initiative, reliance on market mechanisms and trust in the virtues of the "invisible hand" that regulates relations between people, are considered to be the only forms that allow the existence of a society able to ensure our prosperity.

Professor Francis Fukuyama -an American citizen of Japanese origin- maintains (no more no less) that the humanity has arrived at the end point of its sociocultural evolution and at the final form of the human government. He argues: "What we may be witnessing is not just the end of the Cold War, or the passing of a particular period of post-war history, but the end of history as such..." Otherwise, the humanity has passed from the primitive-communal order through slavery, feudalism and capitalism, reaching the today's 'American-style' democracy, presented by Francis Fukuyama as the only 'correct' political system.

In essence the neoliberalism tells us: you who are able, enrich up! And thus, all seven billion people on earth (compared with about 1.6 billion, existing in 1900) will do well! Is it really so?!

First, let us see how the present situation was reached. Although many people will look at us with evil eyes, we have to refer again to Marxism. Rightly, Marx argues that the means of production (tools, machines, factories, infrastructure, science, technology etc.) represent the most dynamic part of the mode of production, and they determine in fact the character of the economic and social order. To make a long story short, is enough if we specify that Soviet-style socialist regimes (today they are called communist regimes) became a powerful brake on the improvement of means of production. Just remember a minor event, but eloquent. In some countries in Eastern Europe, it was almost impossible to have a simple typewriter, it had to be registered at the 'militia' (police) with the sample of the respective characters. That while in Western capitalist countries, with the development of computers in the years 1950-1960 the Internet origins appeared, and there was no problem to have a printer and to communicate electronically with other owners of such equipment located at distances of thousands kilometers.

In the Manifesto of Marx and Engels it is said ironically: "It has been objected that upon the abolition of private property, all work will cease, and universal laziness will overtake us". "All work" did not cease, but the following saying became a reality in the former "communist" countries: "we make them believe that we work, they make believe that they pay us". Consider another quote of the Manifesto: "Modern Industry has converted the little workshop of the patriarchal master into the great factory of the industrial capitalist. Masses of labourers, crowded into the factory, are organised like soldiers. As privates of the industrial army they are placed under the command of a perfect hierarchy of officers and sergeants. Not only are they slaves of the bourgeois class, and of the bourgeois State; they are daily and hourly enslaved by the machine, by the overlooker, and, above all, by the individual bourgeois manufacturer himself". It is clear that they erroneously relied on these "privates of the industrial army" subjected, by the rigors of industrial production, to military discipline. Obviously, their specific cultural and scientific training did not allow these poor "industrial soldiers" to lead efficiently in a society of overall technological progress.

Instead, the Western capitalism and especially the American-style capitalism (the most dynamic of all types of capitalism until now), did match all requirements and profited fully by the rapid progress of means of production that took place during the twentieth century.

Economic and social inequality of world countries

In our world did not exist and there is not any type of society where everything is in the pink. Especially in the last few years, there are a series of unsettling economic and social phenomena. What kind of world is in existence on our planet, if in 2010 the Gross Domestic Product (GDP) per capita in Qatar was $ 90,149 and $ 342 in Congo. Consequently, on average, the population of one of the two countries is over 263 times poorer than the other country's population. What fault have the poorest people on earth, that they were born in a country called Congo? They are not the

10

creations of God as well? Even bigger inequality exists within all countries, whether they are rich or poor.

The "end of history as such" foreseen by Professor Francis Fukuyama and the assessment according to which in the future will be no changes in socio-economic organization of mankind, appear to be contradicted by recent mass protests in Greece, Iceland, Spain, Italy, England, France, Germany, Portugal, Ireland etc.. In the past there were unexpected changes in society. Then, why should we believe that in the future will not be new surprises and that the present organization of society is eternal?

The neoliberalism makes the rich even richer, and impoverish the poor

Even in the United States, the most advanced country in the world and the only superpower, there are signs that portend changes in future. In September 17, 2011, "Occupy Wall Street" ('OWS') protests started in New York City and they have incited similar protests in numerous cities and communities in United States, and all over the world as well. They are caused by today's economic and social inequality, high unemployment rates, greed, as well as the corruption and the undue influence of the corporations, banks and other financial services on the governments.

The American protesters' slogan is "We are the 99%!". In fact this slogan makes reference to the fact that today there is immense income and wealth inequality in the U.S. between the 99% of the population and the wealthiest 1%. From 1970 to 2010, the annual U.S. income share of the top 1% of Americans grew, from about 10% to nearly 25%. After the Recession started in 2007, the share of total wealth owned by the top 1% of the Americans grew from 34.6% to 37.1%, and that owned by the top 20% grew from 85% to 87.7%. Financial inequality is even greater, with the top 1% of the population owning more than 42% of it In fact, during the new Great Recession, the gap between the 1% and the 99% of the U.S. population was further widened. Today, eighty percent of the Americans own less than 13% of the total national wealth!

The American Dream was based on the idea that the United States was considered a country of all possibilities, one that has given endless opportunities for everyone. A "promised land", which provided opportunities for prosperity for all hardworking people. We think it's time to give a small example of how these opportunities were used. By 1910, the grandfather of one of the authors of this essay left for America, from his village situated somewhere in Transylvania (a province of Austria-Hungary at that time). Though he had only two primary classes, working hard, he managed to save some money. So, returning to his homeland after nearly 25 years, with his dollars bought land and became one of the most wealthy men in the village. The author in question, between 1970-1975, worked as an employee of an American computer manufacturing company. At first in research and development in the United States and then in the marketing subsidiary in Vienna (Austria). With the money saved as an employee of the U.S. company, he could build a comfortable apartment in Bucharest. In 1991, his son with a better training in ITC than his father, went to America too. After several years, he became an American citizen. He is currently still working in the computer field. Surprisingly, after over 21 years in the United States, he still lives in a rented house and owes banks (on 'Credit cards') nearly $ 90,000. You would have expected him to become an prosperous man. Through his professional training and because he is serious and hardworking, it would have been normal for him to overcome his father, and the grandfather even more. Maybe, the real reasons that led to this abnormality is precisely the reasons supported by the protests "Occupy Wall Street". It seems that today, in United States do not exist anymore the same opportunities for all, but only for the rich.

The public debt

In recent years, have increased significantly the government debts (public debts) -borrowed usually by issuing securities, government bonds and bills, or borrowed directly from supranational organizations (World Bank, EU) or international financial institutions (IMF) by the less creditworthy countries. The public debt of certain countries reached a level close to that of GDP, or even exceeded it. In 2010, in relation to its

GDP, Japan's public debt was 197.5%, in Greece was 144.9%, in Italy 118.4%, in Ireland 94.9 and 93.3% in Portugal. In 2011, the Gross Federal Debt of U. S. was about $15,500 billion (102% of GDP), of which $9,900 billion is due to companies and individuals. It should be noted that this increase in debt in recent years did not cause ordinary people's lives to improve, but led to their lower standard of living.

Gone are some of the labor rights earned in the past

We can see that after the Russian Bolshevik revolution, in Western countries has been a considerable expansion of the middle class. Strangely, after the dismantling of the USSR and after the collapse of the Eastern bloc, the occidental middle class -including the American middle class- show signs that it gradually began to melt. We do not know if this phenomenon was not coincidental. It can be assumed however that during the existence of the Eastern bloc, those who had and have power in the West ("The Establishment") granted certain advantages to the majority placed at the lower end of the social scale, as to avoid their contamination by leftist ideologies, especially by the communist ideology. With the disappearance of the communist threat, it was considered that these concessions have become unnecessary and even useless. Some leading European economists estimate that there is currently a strong imbalance in the 'labor - capital' relationship. Already, gone are many of the labor rights, earned by heavy fighting during the nineteenth century and consolidated during the twentieth century. Misled are those who argue that regarding the distribution of 'surplus value' (or of value added), there wasn't and there is no significant competing interests between labor and capital. Especially in the last twenty years, the existing distribution favors the capital increasingly, while the labor is seriously harmed.

We believe that regarding the 'surplus value', Marx unduly exaggerated the role and importance of the industrial proletariat. Although indirectly, just as important a role in creating 'added value' have the education and health. The same can be said even about the police and justice. Without them it would be a chaos that would not create any added value. These considerations do not lessen the importance of this issue and is absolutely necessary to recover and rebalance the distribution of 'surplus value' between labor and capital. The 'status quo' would preserve the conditions for the rich to become richer, while others to become more poor. This would result, whether we want it or not, to re start the class struggle between the rich (increasingly fewer) and the poor (increasingly more numerous). Especially when we came to seven billion people and the planet's resources are depleting increasingly faster.

Human greed and individualism do not disappear

The today society is essentially based on human greed and individualism. "If I am well-off, may the world perish!" This has gained universal spreading. We know that by its nature, man tends to accumulate more and more wealth. He will never get enough to satisfy his greed. Actually translates into life the saying that "your appetite comes eating", meaning that as man becomes richer, he gets increasingly eager to grab more and more new wealth. Human nature has not changed much with the passing centuries and there are no signs that it will change in the foreseeable future. But the situation (socio-economic, demographic and environmental) reached today by the mankind, could cause quite unexpected changes.

It is unlikely that mankind will continue indefinitely to accept the coexistence of misery (which expands to more and more people) with the richness and opulence of a tiny minority. The deepening polarization of our society is a matter contrary to Christian morality. Unfortunately, from the Christianity we accept only those parts that are agreeable to each of us. We think about our neighbor only in theory and we care very little if he is starving. When we look around us, almost anywhere in the world, we realize that there is no truth in the slogan of the French Revolution (Liberty, equality, fraternity). An U.S. citizen told us recently that in the world of ours "you are free only if you have money". What kind of equality (even if only legal) exists between a beggar and a millionaire? The saying that "the well fed wealthy does not believe the guy who is starving" is absolutely realistic and demonstrates that there is no true brotherhood in the world.

How wonderful are the following words in The Declaration of Independence: "We hold these truths to be self-evident, that all men are created equal, that they are endowed by their Creator with certain unalienable Rights, that among these are Life, Liberty and the pursuit of Happiness". But, is a man who was born into a family that owns banks, factories and oil wells, "created equal" with another man, who was born into a family that does not have any capital and must sell his workmanship for a living?!

For most people, if not all, "the pursuit of Happiness" is an illusory endeavor to become rich. Traveling "from California to the New York Island", and from Niagara Falls to Key West, we did not discover even a single man, that really would not want to be rich, because "it is easier for a camel to go through the eye of a needle than for a rich man to enter the kingdom of God."

We ask ourselves, what would happen if we would start to convince, in all seriousness, all the wealthy people of the world to implement the following exhortations of Jesus of Nazareth: "Do not store up for yourselves treasures on earth..."; "...go and sell all your possessions and give the money to the poor, and you will have treasure in heaven."; "...lend to them without expecting to get anything back..."; "You cannot serve both God and Money." and "If someone slaps you on the right cheek, offer the other cheek also." Certainly, they would send us urgently to the madhouse!

Kindness, love of your neighbor and the other New Testament teachings lead to the heavenly paradise. To arrive at what is considered to be the earthly paradise with its wealth, you need efficiency, capacity to cope with ruthless competition, greed, aggression and all the means allowed by the law or by your courage. If you are a gentleman, it is enough to apply the following principle: "Just be as nice as you can to everyone, but take their money!." Today, not only people but even countries behave in such a way, that you would think truth can be found in the statement that: "All men are created greedy".

Serious consequences of environmental degradation

Craving for enrichment at any cost and longing for profit by any means (legal and less legal), are the main causes that led to the current serious environmental degradation. Ozone depletion and the greenhouse effect, melting the ice caps at the poles, the increasing pollution of groundwaters, of rivers, seas and oceans, contamination of soil and of its fruits and of the air we breathe, the brutal cutting of forests and drastic reduction of green areas and parks and many other aspects of the environmental degradation have grave consequences on people's lives. Perhaps nowhere do we realize how seriously has been the nature assaulted, than when we go to visit the rivers and lakes we used to swim as teenagers. In one case, in those times the river water was crystal clear and up to three meters deep. Cattle and horses drank from the river. All summer the children were bathing and swimming and the peasants were washing their laundry. Today when we revisit the mentioned river (which is somewhere in Transylvania) you feel a deep sadness, as the water is only up to the ankles, has a bad stench, the river became a sort of sewage canal with sewage waste waters! On it even plastic bags and containers are floating. Such a degradation occurred during the life of a single generation!

Depletion of raw materials and of non-renewable energy resources

Deposits of mineral raw materials and of oil and gas reserves are exploited ruthlessly. We don't consider that something has be left to future generations too. Disproportionate and unsustainable in the future is the energy consumption per capita in the various countries. For example, the U.S. population is about 5% of the world population, but it consumes about 25% of energy on the planet. If India would also have the same per capita energy consumption, nothing would remain for the rest of world population. If in all countries of the planet, would be the same number of cars per thousand people as in the U.S., then in the world it would be over 5 billion cars. In such an event, the world oil deposits would be exhausted in a few years. The populations of the BRIC countries (Brazil, Russia, India and China), legitimately aspire to a Western standard of living. Will there be sufficient resources on the planet Earth, if they will reach the same food consumption, the same equipment endowment in their houses and the same consuming habits? The other countries of Africa, Asia and Latin America have the same hopes! Can they be met in case the "Statu quo" will be maintained?!

After the collapse of the USSR and of the Eastern bloc, the peoples of the world have expected that the military conflicts between countries would disappear, or at least, their number would be reduced. This has not happened. Wars have continued to consume significant financial funds and to cause damages. In the middle of 2011, the news agency "AFP" related that, according to a study published by Brown University, the conflicts involving the United States from 09.11.2000, have killed at least 225,000 people (and about 365,000 wounded) and generated costs of over 3,700 billion dollars. The costs, damages and losses of the other countries, are not known.

Consequences of technological progress

Technological progress, increasingly faster and faster, hasn't only beneficial consequences. Let us recall the discoveries related to uses of nuclear energy. Thus, atomic power plants by themselves are dangerous (the Chernobyl and Fukushima cases can neither be forgotten nor underrated), in addition they are the result of a technology which produces atomic bombs as well. Given that this kind of weapons have been used in the past, no one can guarantee that they will not be used in future! There is danger of using nuclear weapons by terrorists. It would have been better and safer if nuclear power had not been discovered! Notice that no matter how negative are the consequences of such discoveries, they just can't be overlooked and humanity no longer can get rid of them.

The fact that mankind has reached a critical moment, results also from the following quotes from some of the great thinkers. Thus, Albert Einstein said: "We shall require a substantially new manner of thinking if mankind is to survive." At the end of last century, Loren C. Eiseley said: "If the human race is to survive into the next century, scientific technology will have to learn how to control the devastating forces it has unwittingly turned loose on the planet - the world's exploding population, the reckless pollution of the environment, the spiraling arms race and the expenditure of irreplaceable energy". Noam Chomsky said: "If we continue to produce energy by combustion, the human race isn't going to survive much".

Crucial role of capital

In today world of neoliberalism, the importance of capital increases by the day. Instead, along with the progress of ICT (Information and Communications Technology), the importance of labor diminishes continuously. Gradually, factories and plants will be run by the artificial intelligence of computers. They will be operated without personnel, i.e. without any labor. In 'research and development', a relatively small number of highly qualified people will conceive factories, in which the production (including maintenance) will be performed by machines controlled by computers, thus thousands of workers of traditional industries of the past will be eliminated. Such automation have appeared in other areas of the economy as well. As a result of this phenomenon, it became already more and more difficult to find jobs. All over the world, when you get a job is considered that you got a favor. A gift that you got from those who own the capital. As time goes by, will be fewer and fewer jobs, most of them will be in service industry. In the long run, the classical industrial proletariat will disappear altogether.

So far, economic efficiency could be achieved only in countries where there existed an immense income and wealth inequality. In China (led by the Chinese Communist Party), Mao's egalitarianism was abandoned and passed to the "socialist market economy" (or just plain capitalism) of Teng Xio Peng. He said: "It does not matter whether they are black cats or white cats; so long as they catch mice, they are good cats". Following these radical changes in China, today there is an income and wealth inequality just as great as in the West. Obviously only in this way, it was possible to modernize China and to obtain an extraordinary rate of GDP growth.

When a country exceeds a certain level of development, efficiency does not depend anymore on the inequality of income and wealth distribution, but on the ICT and the computers that operate and manage the economy (including industry). This means that already is possible to achieve economic efficiency, even when there is no inequality in income and wealth distribution. Hence, the gap between the rich and the vast majority of world population can be stopped. As required by a great poet, "the cruel and unjust social order that divides the world into rich and paupers!" can be crushed!

The world population will reach ten billion in fewer years than we think, so it is absolutely necessary to cancel the huge difference between rich and poor countries. In the past century, occured the collapse and final dismemberment of all the European colonial empires (Portuguese, Spanish, French, British, German, Dutch, Belgian, Italian, etc.). Ottoman,

Habsurg and Russian empires collapsed also. Hitler's "thousand years grossdeutsches reich" lasted only 12 years. The Soviet Empire, created by Lenin and Stalin, collapsed unexpectedly. Only an Mr. Gorbachev was needed for that! Maybe now is the time, for the economic neocolonialism to be crushed, as in our times, some of the old colonial powers hinder in fact, the development of the other backward countries, even inside the European Union. That there is truth in this, will be proved in the following case study.

B - *Case Study: Romania After 22 Years of Neoliberalism*

Why did we choose Romania as a case study? Because we the authors of this essay are Romanian citizens, and the neoliberalism did not cause such significant and lasting consequences in other countries, as it did in Romania.

As we know, starting with December 1989, Romania has started on the path of abrupt and fundamental changes. This is not the first time when this country, willy-nilly, has taken such a path. But, these changes and transformations had produced so many losses in the industry and economy of this country, like never before. To convince us of the reality of this assertion, it is sufficient to cross the territory of Romania by train and to look from the railway car's window. Everywhere the eye can see factories and plants with blackened and broken windows, former livestock stables with part of the walls remaining, agricultural land overgrown with weeds... Portions of the railroad has reached a derelict stage and the speed of the train you are in is lower than it was just after the First World War. Average speed of fast trains in Romania is about 57 km / hour. In France the average speed of 'TGV' trains is over 263 km / hour! In cities, almost all banks, all the supermarkets and hypermarkets have names of which can be deduced that they don't belong anymore to native people.

Romanian history revealed that, sometimes the

leaders of this country 'were more Catholic than the Pope'. In the aftermath of the Second World War, the leaders of Romania proved to be 'more communist than Stalin'. After December 1989, the Romanian leaders (most of them former zealous members of the Romanian Communist Party) wanted to show the world that they were 'more capitalist than Rockefeller'! The adopted solutions have been, in many ways, more radical and more neoliberal than those applying in other countries of the former Eastern bloc. Because of this, from 1990 to present time, in Romania have been a number of records which manifest themselves in reverse than should be in a normal economy.

Incredible records in Romania

a) *Minimum records that should be maximum*
Today we are witnessing in Romania at the lowest funds allocated for infrastructure, at the lowest budgetary allocations for education, health and research and also at the lowest crop yields and at the lowest efficiency in the livestock sector.

Romania recorded the lowest revenue from tourism, the smaller funds drawn from the European Union, the fewest motorways and upgraded roads and the fewest social housing.

Finally, there is the lowest wages and pensions, lowest welfare, lowest child benefit and consequently the lowest life expectancy.

b) *Maximum records that should be minimum*

The last three years, we are witnessing at the biggest economic collapse in Romania, at the largest program of destruction of the national economy, at the gravest corruption, smuggling and tax evasion, at the greatest destruction of the domestic banking system, at the highest increase of VAT and at the most rural destruction.

In comparison with other EU countries, in Romania have been the biggest layoffs of teachers and doctors, the largest increase in poverty rate and the largest number of employees living in poverty, the highest percentage of families that can not cover current expenses, largest cut in the pay of budgetary employees and the largest population migration, especially of the young people. In Romania, the largest number of jobs have been lost, the most uncultivated farmland is recorded, there is the highest interest rate of the Central Bank, the largest increase in foreign debt, the largest price increase and the highest inflation.

No wonder that in this country the largest school drop is recorded, the most illiterate persons, the most schools closed, the most diseases of poverty and the highest infant mortality rate.

We can "boast" the highest records in Europe, materialized in the political incapacity of the government, in the highest number of central and local leaders who are corrupt and disconnected from reality, and the highest concern of government to make laws against its own people and of the state called Romania.

"Original" neoliberal solutions applied in Romania

To show that in Romania it was as nowhere else, we will refer to several specific examples.

In Romania the large agricultural farms were sprayed in millions of small plots. Today, the 10 million hectares of arable land in the country is divided into 48 million plots. In this country it is the smallest average agricultural holding in the European Union, i.e. of 3.5 hectares. In Hungary, Czech Republic, Slovakia and the former GDR were kept the existing large farms of former 'agricultural cooperatives'. Small plots of agricultural land don't allow the use of present machinery and the practice of modern agricultural methods, this is one of the reasons that in Romania productions of wheat per hectare are usually half as in Hungary. Although Romania's fertile lands have the potential to feed a population of 80 million inhabitants (i.e., four times more than existing residents), it was reached the case that the great part of the food should be imported. Unlike this situation, Norway, in spite of its long winters and rocky land, does not import half of this percentage.

We will compare on how Hungarians have done in the oil field. Although Hungary does not have oil deposits worthy of being taken into account, for the Hungarian 'MOL' oil company a price of 20 billion dollars was offered. But because of strategic considerations, the Hungarians refused to sell it. In contrast, Romania agreed to collect, at the privatization of 'Petrom', the amount of 668 million euros as the price for 51% of its shares. That is to say, for a fraction of the price the Hungarians were offered, Romania lost control over its main oil company. Extremely damaging is the royalty established over a period of 10 years for the oil and gas extracted in Romania. The Romanian State receives between 6 and 8% of the worth of the extraction; at the time when this damaging contract was signed, Libya received between 80 and 85%! In fact, nowhere in the world is charged a royalty so low as that for the gas and the crude oil extracted in Romania.

'Rompetrol' Company, who owned the 'Midia' refinery (most modern in South East Europe) and which had Libyan claims worth $ 80 million, was privatized on 66 million dollars. The Romanian President and the Prime Minister during that time (party leaders said to be of social-democratic orientation) have approved the privatization of 'Rompetrol' to be made in favor of one rival political leader belonging to the Liberal Party. This is proof that in Romania, all politicians are interconnected by common interests, and sharing their left or right parties is purely formal. Prevail only their personal interests! After a while, the new local owner sold 'Rompetrol' to 'KazMunaiGaz' a company owned by the Kazakhstan State; only 75% of the shares being valued at $ 3.6 billion.

O subject of controversy is the ancient gold mines 'Rosia Montana' privatization deal. For 20 years lease of of 520 square kilometers of land, the 'Gold Corporation' Company pays to the Romanian state only $ 20,000 per year. If the privatization will be concluded, the Romanian state will receive 15% of benefits, and 'Gold Corporation' the remaining 85%. Operation and providing jobs will last only 17 years, in that period will be extracted all existing gold, silver, uranium, wolfram etc. There will be beheaded four mountains, and after the mining will remain a lake filled with an enormous amount of cyanide water; a possible earthquake could cause havoc not only in Romania but also in Hungary. Dacian and Roman galleries mining sites, dating back over 2,000 years, will disappear. It is known that the Roman Emperor Trajan restored the finances of the empire with the gold extracted from the 'Rosia Montana' mines. During the Roman Empire were extracted circa 500 tonnes of gold. Within centuries, the Hapsburg Empire took advantage, as well, of the gold extracted from these mines (over 800 tons). But even the Roman Empire and the Habsburgs have something left to the next generations. This time, they no longer intend to leave something to the descendants of the poor Romanians; will be extracted everything and it is only in favor of a company from a very rich country, namely in Canada. The Dacians, the Romans, or even less the Habsburgs, did not give others the right to remove gold from the mines at 'Rosia Montana'! Instead, Romanian government officials (ardent followers of neoliberalism) strive and endeavor to sell cheap these deposits, which are the richest in Europe both in gold, as well as in silver, uranium, wolfram and other rare metals.

We mention that, although they are extracted from the publications and media statements, might be that the figures given in this chapter and the rest of the essay to be erroneous. This for the simple reason that all post-December Revolution governments have made sure that, big business and privatization contracts are confidential. Although it was the trading of goods and wealth of the Romanian state, the Romanian citizens (nominal owners of Romania, under the Constitution) were not allowed to know the ins and outs of contracts. It is not hard to guess why they acted in such a manner and why they proceed further in this way.

What caused the collapse of the Romanian agriculture and industry

A synthetic definition, including the causes that brought this country in its present situation is given by one of the greatest contemporary Romanian historians who stated that: "The post-December political class is the most incompetent, the most greedy and arrogant in Romanian history. Lacking expertise, hungry for money-making and secure of impunity, this political class fell on Romania with only one thought: to get rich. They have robbed (the country); even more than the much blamed phanariots did. Today, we see that the industry is liquidated, the agriculture is crashed to the ground, the health system is in collapse, the education is in crisis, Romania's international individuality has disappeared." The comparison with the "much blamed phanariots", i.e. with those sent in the old times by the Turkish Sultans to administer the Romanian Principalities, is entirely realistic.

The seriousness of the situation reached by Romania results from the following statement made, in October 2010, by the current leader of the main ruling party and former Prime Minister: "The Liberal Democratic Party had the misfortune to take over government in the worst period of the last 60 years." In other words, he said that Romania is going through an even more difficult period, than during the communist dictatorship!

In what follows are three categories of laws, adopted in accordance with the sacrosanct doctrine of neoliberalism, which led Romania to reach the current situation.

a) On February 19, 1991, was adopted the Land Law no. 18, which liquidated agricultural production cooperatives, together with their fixed facilities and resources. Afterwards, was adopted the legislation that led to the liquidation of the former State Farms ('IAS'), of the Agricultural Machinery and Tractors Companies ('SMT') and of the State Complexes for raising cattle, pigs and poultry and, also to the liquidation of the commercial organizations dealing with collection, storage and marketing of plant and animal agricultural products.

The consequences were disastrous. The peasants, allotted millions of small plots of land, had no equipment and financial funds necessary for the application of modern agricultural technologies. In many parts of Romania farmers are working today as in Middle Ages, with plows pulled by oxen, cows or horses. Another telling example is that, in 2011, large quantities of melons of 'Dăbuleni' (most tasty in Europe) had rotted, because nothing was created to replace the former state enterprises for the marketing of agricultural products. The "invisible hand" that regulates the market did not act to the benefit of Romanian farmers; melons from Spain and Greece were heavily imported, although they are less tasty and more expensive.

The agriculture was sprayed in millions of small plots and irrigation on most of the 3 million hectares was destroyed. Were annihilated agriculture upstream connections (practically has disappeared the fabrications of agricultural machinery, tractors and trucks, were brought close to bankruptcy the agricultural research stations, so instead of producing in the country, much of plant and animal varieties are imported). And downstream connections, as well (have been closed many food plants, and in some that still exists, milk and yogurt are produced with milk powder imported from Germany). Romania, that used to be a net exporting country of agricultural products, reached in some years to import 70% of food in urban consumption. In supermarkets and hypermarkets in Romania (of French, German, Greek and Austrian property) even apples, pears, potatoes, garlic and peaches are imported from Greece, Germany, France, Austria, Hungary, Turkey and China. Before 1990, shops in Vienna and other Austrian and German cities were full of Romanian peaches. In recent years, Romania exported agricultural raw materials (i.e. corn, wheat and sunflower seeds), instead importing foods with high added value.

On agricultural research, suffice is it to say that the 'Research Institute for Agriculture and Rural Economy' works today with only 14 researchers, compared with 190 before December 1989. In perspective it is envisaged that the remaining 14 researchers will be laid off, and so this institution of national importance for Romania will be abolished. And this, in a country with 13.289 million hectares of agricultural land and where, in theory, they say that the agriculture is a basic branch of the national economy.

Another significant example is the case of the bankruptcy and liquidation of the 'Comtim' Pig Raising Complex, which before December 1989 was a major exporter and one of the most modern and largest pork producers in the world. Today, Romania became a net importer of pork, while Romanian pork covers only 30 percent of domestic consumption.

b) The privatization and restitution laws adopted after December 1989 and how they were applied, had similar disastrous consequences.

In the 22 years since the Revolution, in Romania there was a continuous process of deindustrialization. Most of the factories and plants, mostly created during the 'communist' period by sacrificing several generations, have been bankrupted and have reached "scrap iron heaps". Many of them were literally dismantled and exported as scrap metal! The industries of steel, aluminum, cement, petroleum (including the crude oil and associated gas deposits on land and sea), fixed telephony, electrical and gas distributions and almost all banks, have been sold cheep to foreigners.

Were abolished most of the research and development institutes, and those that survive remain with a reduced staff.

The disaster was also a consequence, of all sorts of thievery, robbery and of widespread corruption.

For now we will give only a few significant examples that will show what followed the adoption of the aforementioned legislations.

'Sidex Galati' Company was one of the largest integrated steel plants in the world. It was designed to achieve a production of 10 million tons / year of steel (approximately 30,000 steel grades) and to produce millions of tons of rolled steel and various types of metallurgical coke and coke chemical products (coal tar etc.). It was equipped with modern machinery and technology imported from the West (Germany, France, Japan etc.). According to reports of mass media, 'Sidex Galati' was privatized at a price below the value of raw materials existing at that time in the company. Now the former 'Sidex Galati' Company is only a strip mill, the coke oven and the blast furnaces have ceased to function.

In 1989, the Romanian steel industry produced about 14 million tons of steel and more than 9 million tons of iron; in this area the country occupied one of the front places in Europe. Today in Romania there is no steel industry. It was 'privatized' and abolished even the ancient 'Reşiţa Steel Works', which -at the time when it was part of Austro-Hungarian Empire- delivered the steel bars with which the famous Eiffel Tower in Paris was built. After privatization, in 'Târgovişte Special Steel Works', the machinery and the equipment components of one of its sections, were transferred abroad. Other sections now looks like after bombing, not only the equipment came to scrap iron but even some of the bars in the concrete walls.

In the year 1978, negotiations were held regarding the construction of the classic part of the ' Cernavoda Nuclear Power Plant'. On that occasion, the 'IMGB Company' ('Bucharest Heavy Machinery Company') was visited and evaluated (on the possibilities of integration of that power equipment) by a 'General Electric' delegation of specialists, headed by a senior vice president from its headquarters in USA. He said that, at that time, the famous 'General Electric Company' did not have a plant so well equipped with machine tools as the Romanian 'IMGB Company'. In the 1997-1998 privatization campaign "on a dollar", the 'IMGB Company' was privatized. Subsequently, the Norwegian-British corporation (the new owner) sold the 'IMGB' canteen-club, obtaining a much higher price than that paid for buying the entire industrial giant.

The privatization of the 'Upetrom 1 Mai Company' from Ploiesti was considered a success. In the aftermath of World War II, thanks to this plant, Romania became the third largest producer of oil rigs in the world (after USA and USSR) and the second largest exporter (after U.S.). It was the second largest producer and exporter of roller drill bits (after U.S.). 'Upetrom 1 Mai' reached 24,000 personnel. Today it has only 3,000 employees. Visiting 'Upetrom 1 Mai Company' some time ago, it was found that they were only repairing some mud pumps. The former section of manufacturing roller drill bits, completely ceased its activity. Technical equipment of the company were the same as 30-40 years ago.

The 'ARO' off-road vehicles were exported to many countries. They could be seen even in the Latin American soap operas presented on TV. Some years ago, in newspapers and on television, there were long discussions on the 'ARO' privatization scandal and the resulting damages. Then everything was forgotten. The production of the 'ARO' off-road vehicles stopped forever. No longer are produced in Romania trucks, buses, trolleybuses, locomotives, grain transporting railway cars, machine tools (automatic lathes etc), although, years ago, they were successfully exported to Arab countries, China, USSR, Latin America and U.S.

'Tractorul Brasov' Company was one of the biggest manufacturers and exporters of tractors in Europe. In exchange for deliveries of oil, this company had an assembly line in Iran for 10,000 tractors per year.

Gradually after 1990, 'Tractorul Brasov' Company was bankrupted. At a time, in one of its buildings, mattresses were produced. Then, its goods were auctioned and on the territory of 'Tractorul Brasov' Company a residential neighborhood and a shopping center will be built.

Also, due to the privatization laws, Romania's merchant fleet (the seventh largest in the world) was volatilized. The ocean fishing fleet disappeared as well, which after that of the Soviet Union was the largest of those operating in the Atlantic Ocean. Huge financial funds had been spent to buy those ships and trawlers, and that had been done during the "communist" regime, by the sacrifice of the standard of living of the Romanian population.

The main state banks were privatized and they became subsidiaries of large Austrian, French and Greek banks. Today, over 90% of the banking capital in Romania is owned by foreigners. Such a high proportion of the banking capital to be owned by the foreigners, there is not existing in none of the neighboring countries and even in none of the former colonies in Africa, Asia and Latin America.

Through 7 branches of the Greek banks, Greece holds today 27% of the banking capital in Romania. There are similar, substantial Greek participation in the retail trade, in food industry, mineral waters, etc. In favor of Greek operator OTE, the 'Romtelecom' Company was privatized, which at that time had the monopoly for fixed telephony in Romania. The analysis and debates of the Senate investigative committee, has shown that so-called privatization has meant, in fact, the transfer of ownership from the Romanian state to the Greek state, the selling price of $675 million being well below the actual value of the Romanian telephone network; they say that, a percentage of 10% as a secret commission was received i.e. 67 million dollars. Parliamentary debates proved a waste of time, they have not led to any action, everything was forgotten.

Recently, at a scientific event held in Bucharest, a renowned Greek economist, was worried about the fact that Germany and other rich northern countries in European Union, taking advantage of the debt crisis, are trying to seize the Greek banks and enterprises; the ultimate goal being "ruining the Greek economy and enslaving the Greeks to foreigners". Of course, protesting strongly against such a probable future event, that Greek economist forgot to mention that the seizure and ruin of the Romanian economy was already realized in the past tense, and at that specific action Greece had substantially participated.

Almost all the insurance and reinsurance in Romania came under the control of foreign companies. In 2007, the Austrian insurance company 'Vienna Insurance Group' - 'VIG' in Vienna, became majority shareholder in the ancient Romanian 'Asirom' Company. Before, 'Asirom' had the insurance monopoly in Romania.

In Romania retrocessions were not and are not limited. A large part of Transylvania became the property of foreigners. Billions of dollars and euros have been sent out of the country, because retrocessions had no limited values, as is the case in neighboring countries (Hungary, Czech Republic, etc.). For example, a factory was privatized and the Romanian State received a price of $ 5 million, then the Romanian government had to compensate the foreign descendants of the previous owner with 300 million euros!

In Hungary, real estates were not returned to anyone (neither to Hungarian 'Grofs' and neither to Hapsburg descendants - their former royal family). In Romania they returned to 'Grofs' and foreign royal families (Habsburg and Hohenzollern-Sigmaringen), palaces, thousands of hectares of forests and huge estates. Though this country has very few buildings of that kind, there have been returned to those royal families the famous 'Peles' castles and the 'Bran Dracula Castle'.

Based on the calculations of economists, as a consequence of all these legislations, which were based literally on the principles of neoliberalism, Romania's national heritage was injured with circa 2,000 billion dollars. If you divide this figure to the current stable population of Romania, this represents over 105,000 U.S. dollars per capita. Real damage is even greater if we consider what could have produced and how many jobs would have existed in all these factories, works, agricultural breeding complexes, land irrigations and the other patrimonies destroyed or sold cheep to foreigners. Have been proved futile the cruel sacrifices of the Romanians, due to the forced industrialization of the communist dictatorship! The today youngsters and the future generations will inherit an impoverished Romania. And for all this enormous damage it was not found nobody to blame. No one has said even a simple "mea culpa"!

Some of the "foreign investments in Romania", were actually pseudo-investments

The above mentioned legislations have determined, every year, a drastic reduction in investments. In addition, much of the investments registered statistically as 'foreign investments in Romania', were actually pseudo-investments. They were made using the formula shown below.

Suppose that a manufacturing company created before December 1989 by investing hundreds of millions of dollars, was privatized in favor of a foreign company for tens of millions of euros. This money was reported statistically as "foreign investment" in Romania. After taking over the company, the new owner stopped production and exported all machinery as scrap metal. Then, sold the land to build a shopping center or a residential neighborhood. In this way, the new owner not only recovered the price paid for privatization, but usually get a profit several times higher than the amount "invested". Certainly, the main purpose of the foreign company that made this pseudo-investment was not to achieve production in Romania, but to get rid of a competition and to capture the Romanian market for the products manufactured elsewhere.

The media, have presented many cases of this kind. It is enough to remember that, before December 1989, toothpastes and soaps used by the Romanians were almost entirely produced in Romania. One of the major manufacturers was 'Nivea' Brasov Company, which besides soaps and toothpastes had a wide range of products: shaving creams, skin creams, deodorants, sprays, aerosols, shampoos, perfumes, toilet waters and household chemicals. In nearby area, plantations of mint, lavender and sage, were developed on an area of 280 hectares. Because of a good quality-price ratio, 'Nivea' Brasov managed to get full control of the markets in Middle East and Eastern Europe, with its products. After 1990 the firm was renamed 'Norvea'. In 1993, 'Norvea' was privatized, 'Colgate-Palmolive' Company taking 76% of its shares; in 2006 were bought the remaining 24%. After privatization, the production of the 'Norvea' Brasov Company has stopped completely and was transferred to Poland. Today, in Romania toothpastes and soaps are no longer produced. For sure, the forenamed foreign "investor" got a good part of the Romanian market for its products. 'Colgate-Palmolive' still produces some 'Norvea' products in Poland, which are imported into Romania.

Flat tax, impoverish most people

c) The introduction in this country, since January 1, 2005, of a flat tax of 16%, worsened further the standard of living of the lower strata of the population. Of the 27 European Union countries, the flat tax applies only in Romania and in another few countries.

Taxation by the same percentage, both the incomes of the person who received 'Rompetrol' as a gift, and the salary of an employee who is remunerated with minimum wage, is deeply unethical and uneconomical. To compensate for the gap in the national budget resulting from the adoption of flat tax, the consumption taxes that everyone pays (VAT, excise, etc.), were increased. In this way ordinary people, that is the most of the population, are severely disadvantaged. According to calculations by some economists, in the first four years of flat tax, the rich people of Romania were advantaged by the amount of 136.4 billion dollars. The propaganda of those who introduced the flat tax, according to which those billions will be invested in the economy, did not actually been true. In exchange, Romania was filled with luxury cars and houses of hundreds of thousands and even million of euros; the rich people of the transition defy the common people with their arrogance and opulence (purses, dresses, shoes and watches of thousands and tens of thousands of euros). Their luxury consumption (based mainly on services and products purchased from abroad) is stimulated. Instead, consumption of the lower strata of society, represented largely by the services and goods produced in Romania, is drastically reduced. Economic consequences of these facts are obvious for anyone with even minimal macroeconomic knowledge.

Rampant inflation and the collapse of financial and banking system

The rampant inflation after 1990 had an ill-fated role in the impoverishment of the population, and in the de-capitalization of companies, and finally in the demolition of the Romanian economy. We remember the three-digit annual average rates of inflation in 1994 (136.7%) and in 1997 (154.2%). Although in that period, the leadership of the National Bank of Romania (BNR) announced proudly that the macrostabilization of economy was carried out, the phenomenon really got out of control. Actually, by repeated macrostabilization in Romanian style, most of the population become poor and a tiny minority amassed fabulous wealth. Inflation in our country is among the highest in Europe at present too.

In 1997, Professor Anghel N. Rugina, an important Romanian-born American economist, said that the National Bank of Romania "began to give the final blow, all based on the advices given by foreign experts in collaboration with its own advisors, namely by applying the so-called shock therapy." "The application of exorbitant interest rates of 50%, 100%, 200%, 250%, 300%, in the name of macro fiscal and monetary policies, produced an economic and financial disaster of which the Romanian economy could not recover even to this day. Specifically was destroyed completely the formation of real capital, without which no national economy can progress." "The Romanian industry, with its bad sides and good sides as well, have flopped because of the official policy of drastic weakening of the domestic markets and the freezing of real capital formation by exorbitant interest rates. The imported foreign capital or the credit(s) coming from foreign loans were used to cover budget deficits in state finances and (in) balance of international payments, not to stimulate the economy; plus pure speculation on the currency market."

The quotations given in full demonstrate eloquently, the essential causes of the collapse of the Romanian economy. Really, the Romanian economy has not recovered, not even until this year of 2012; if the 'status quo' is maintained, nor will it return in the next 20 years. Contrarily, the situation will get worse.

The National Bank of Romania has its share of blame for the fact that almost all the banking capital and almost all the banks in Romania had gone in the hands of foreign banks. Romania remained virtually without Romanian banks. The 'CEC Bank' (the ancient 'House of Savings') and Eximbank are the only remaining state-owned Romanian banks, but have together a small percentage of the banking market.

There have been forgotten, all under the guidance of the National Bank of Romania, the billions of dollars and of Romanian 'lei' lost or looted from 'Bancorex', 'Agricultural Bank', 'Dacia Felix Bank' etc. There have not been clarified the strange bankruptcy of the following banks: 'Bankcoop', 'Credit-Bank', 'Columna-Bank', 'Romanian Discount Bank' ('BRS'), 'International Bank of Religions' ('BIR'), 'Turkish-Romanian Bank' ('BTR') etc. Although there were debated in the press and at TV, there were not clarified some of the unique "banking businesses" in the world. Thus it was said that one of the owners of the 'Dacia Felix Bank' decided to buy shares worth 160 million dollars, from his own company in Luxembourg. This company being bankrupted, the bank lost the money invested in those shares. In fact, in Switzerland -the country of banks- was published an article entitled "7 lessons for the robbery of a Romanian bank", which shows how that person looted almost 400 million dollars from 'Dacia Felix Bank'. From the confessions of a former president of the 'Romanian Discount Bank' ('BRS'), resulted that it has been practiced some brutal methods of robbery (fictitious credit and use of so-called 'cans' to transfer some funds to the final beneficiaries). It was said that the 'Turkish-Romanian Bank' ('BT) placed over 120 million dollars in foreign banks, then the funds were used as collateral for the loans of the main shareholder.

On television and in the newspapers was stated that a significant portion of the 20 billion loan borrowed in 2009 from the IMF, EU and the World Bank, went straight to the National Bank of Romania, and from there some of the billions reached, by reducing compulsory reserves, the branches of foreign banks in Romania. An ambassador of one of the major countries said: "You borrowed 20 billion euros from the EU and from multinational organizations like the IMF, but you have 20 billion euros in EU funds, expecting you to pull them in your accounts".

On the Internet somebody ascertained that as a rule, under the guidance of the National Bank of Romania, in the first 3-5 months of each year, the currency rate of the Romanian 'lei' against the dollar and the euro rises, so that after holding the general meetings of shareholders, the foreign owners of the companies in Romania can change the Romanian currency in their favor.

There were not clarified the robberies regarding the 'Mutual Fund of Businessmen' ('FMOA') - administered by 'SAFI Invest'- and neither regarding the 'National Investment Fund' ('FNI'). The people to whom important funds reached, have not been disturbed whatsoever. Because of this reason, in the Romanians eyes, the mutual funds have been compromised for a long time. The negative perception was also extended upon the stock exchange and upon the commodity markets. Due to these reasons, in Romania, the amounts invested in mutual funds as well as market capitalization of the stock exchange are negligible; they have virtually no influence on the country's economic development.

Romania's tourism potential

Romania has a significant tourism potential, of which we mention: the 'Apuseni' Mountains - known abroad as the 'Transylvanian Alps', the Carpathians, the Black Sea, the Danube Delta - unique in Europe, the medieval towns of Transylvania, the Bucovina's picturesque monasteries and the wooden churches of Maramures. But because of the precarity of transport infrastructure, smaller countries and less equipped like Hungary, Bulgaria and the Czech Republic host several times more foreign tourists than Romania.

Romania has significant sources of thermal and mineral waters, which today are poorly exploited. Ancient spa-s for medical treatment (Herculane, Borsec, Sovata, Govora, and many others) have been privatized and then left to ruin. It is no use spending huge funds for advertising ("land of choice" and "Carpathian gardens"), if there are no highways and roads, at least at the level of the neighboring countries. Years ago, the country's current President said, while he was Minister of Transportations, that Romania did not need highways! What he said, was fulfilled: there are no highways, and there will not be enough of them, not even in 25 more years. Especially in recent years, major financial funds were spent for swimming pools and parks in villages, gondolas and ski tracks in areas with little snow, etc. The media has shown that in Romania were accepted incomparably higher prices, compared with those in other countries, both in these kind of investments, as well as per kilometer of highway (in the few short sections actually built).

The foreign visitors are discouraged to come to Romania by the low level of services, by the corruption and the chaos found everywhere. The state of chaos existing in Romania came out strongly in the following instance. On July 16, 2011, in the Chitila village (situated 10 km from Bucharest), have been stolen four cases with 80 missile warheads, from a train carrying arms to a company in Sofia - Bulgaria; the warheads were transported from a factory situated at circa 30 km from Brasov. Within the wooden cases there were zinc boxes, and in them the warheads. Each case was weighing about 100 kilograms. On July 18, three cases of 60 warheads were found (intact and sealed) in a drained well in the forest of Chitila. The fourth case was found on a street in Chitila. It was empty and traces of burning of the wooden case could be seen; which looks like it was used fire to open the case, perhaps even oxyacetylene flame. So it was pure luck that, this method of opening the box did not lead to the explosion of the warheads. A total of 19 warheads of this case were found in the forest of Chitila, thrown in a bag. On July 19th, the 80th warhead was found in the same area, in a septic pit; so, it was necessary to empty the mentioned pit for the warhead to be safely removed. Had the warhead exploded during this procedure, among other things, all the surroundings would have been polluted with a specific pestilential smell. The whole story was presented on the TV and it was said also that, the ten Romanian gendarmes who guarded the train carrying arms, had not noticed the stealing of the warheads, because they were watching a soccer match! The engine driver and his helper stopped the train just to steal and sell 75 liters of oil in exchange for 300 RON (About 70 euros)! ROMARM National Company declared that in the export contract was provided a clause according to which the transfer of property was to take place in Brasov; from that moment the responsibility for transport should rest on the Bulgarian beneficiary. This is another enormity! How could the relevant Bulgarian authorities be answerable for the safety of arms transport when the train would cross the Romanian territory from Brasov to Giurgiu (located on the border with Bulgaria)?! This proves again that in Romania is like no place else!

The packs of stray dogs that we meet everywhere in the capital city, the crowds of beggars in all towns and the garbage on the streets and around buildings, even the official ones, also contribute to weak appetite of the foreigners to come to Romania as tourists.

The State, a "bad manager"

In Romania is widespread the idea that the state is a poor administrator. This idea was promoted especially by those who managed and determined the fate of the national patrimony, of the Romanian state. The reality after December 1989, showed that the government officials, MPs and those who were directly answerable for these assets (including of the financial and economic enterprises of the state) had incomes, which were mostly not based on their salaries. It's enough to mention that at some point, the country with the poorest population in the EU had the richest Prime Minister throughout all the Union. Although, before the Revolution of December 1989, because of the egalitarianism of the communist dictatorship, he was just as poor as all the other Romanian citizens. Actually, in the last 22 years, his main occupations were, the following: politician, party leader, minister, prime minister and representative in the parliament. Why do we wonder that, like others in his situation, this particular politician managed to accumulate a considerable fortune?

It is easy to explain the connection between the enrichment with the Romanian reality of privatizations and restitutions, with the fact that the state investments have been made at prices much higher than in other countries. The truth is that only by striving for the legitimate interests of the Romanian state, those officials or decision makers, would have confined themselves to a relatively modest salary. Facilitating privatizations and restitutions in Romanian style, adopting laws 'with dedication', or allowing bid rigging, they could get rich overnight with dozens and even hundreds of million euros.

In Romania, what is stolen, is stolen for good. In vain a former justice minister and former party leader said: "It is unacceptable that those who steal a chicken to be jailed two, three years, and those who steal billions to stay free." And a former prime minister (a son-in-law of two high communist officials, before 89) said serenely: "Except for utilities, all that was attractive was sold or sacked. There is nothing attractive for privatization anymore". A former President of Romania during three periods, rightly said that "an accompanying phenomenon of the transition - ... is corruption and it erodes the structures of the economy and the Romanian society, including the political field (...) corruption entered Justice and Police also". The same President serenely said that in Romania, in fact, was created a "crony capitalism". Given his high positions, certainly, this Mr. President knew what he was speaking about! The result is that after all these statements, pious and critical at the same time, Romania still remains today the most corrupt country in the European Union. However, no important corrupt was ever sentenced until now! A professor of law and a barrister at the same time, said that in Romania it's not likely to be convicted any important corrupt. Once brought to Justice (very rare case), the accused can spend over a million euros, in order to engage a cohort of highly qualified lawyers. Studying hundreds of technical and financial files, they ultimately can prove by 'lawful' evidences that the culprit is 'inocent' and so, the looted millions of euros will remain in the possesion of the corupt. Typically, the money earned in this way are deposited safety in foreign banks. On the Internet, it was published that Romanian citizens have between 30 and 60 billion euros in bank deposits abroad.

Large privatizations in favor of companies controlled by foreign countries

Many Romanians hoped that once Romania joins the EU, on January 1, 2007, the theft and corruption (especially high level corruption) in the country will stop. It was believed that the European Parliament and European Union authorities will require in the new Member State to be instituted a real order and honor. Unfortunately, this did not happen. The other Member States were satisfied with the fact that Romania has become a good market for the goods and services produced in their countries. It seems, that the big countries, which determine in the de facto the rules of the game in the European Union, have been satisfied too. This refers especially to France and Germany who have managed, in addition to seizing a good chunk of the Romanian market, to grab some of the most lucrative natural monopolies of the country (electricity, gas and water distributions, garbage collection). In addition it must be said that, in the year 2010, Romania was the only new member of the European Union in the position of net payer; i.e. the European funds absorption was below the contribution that has to be payed to the EU's budget. In other words, Romania, the poorest country in the European Union subsidizes the living standards of rich citizens of the Union. For these reasons, more and more Romanian citizens believe that it would have been better for them, if Romania wouldn't have joined the European Union.

For motives mentioned in the previous chapter, the rich men of the Romanian transition forget that the biggest privatizations have actually been done with 'strategic' partners having foreign state capital, mainly or even a majority.

The most praised privatization, namely of the 'Dacia' Car Manufacturing Company, has been done with the 'Renault Group' in which the majority of the shares belong to the French state. The privatization of 'Petrom' was been done with 'OMV' in which 35.5% of the shares are owned by the Austrian state and 20% by the Abu Dhabi state. 'Rompetrol' has come entirely in the ownership of 'KazMunaiGaz', which is a state company of Kazakhstan.

The gas distribution monopoly in Romania was assigned to two foreign groups. 'Distrigaz Sud' (46.68% of the gas distributed in the country) was acquired by the 'GDF Suez' Group, whose main shareholder is the French State (35.9% of shares); other shareholders have 5.2% of shares and less (French employees have 2.3% of shares). 'Distrigaz Nord "(47.53% of the gas distributed in the country), was taken over by the German' 'E. ON Ruhrgas' Company in Dusseldorf. The annual gas consumption of Romania is about 17.4 billion cubic meters, of which 6 billion cubic meters is produced by 'Romgaz' (still owned by the Romanian state), 6.3 billion cubic meters is produced by 'Petrom' (belonging to

'OMV' controlled by the Austrian state) and 5.1 billion cubic meters is imported from Russia. Because the import is not made directly, but through intermediaries (Imex Oil, Conef and Wintershal), the price paid by the Romanians is much higher compared to the one paid in Germany and in the rest of Europe. That is the case, although Romania is geographically located nearer the sources of the Russian gas.

Romania has significant resources of unconventional shale gas. In most countries, shale gas extraction is not allowed, because their exploitation (by hydraulic fracturing) represent a serious risk of groundwater pollution. However, the Romanian authorities have already granted licenses to oil companies, Chevron (U.S.), Mol (Hungary) and Energy Assets (Canada), for the prospecting, exploration and exploitation of shale gas in Transylvania and Dobrogea.

Unlike the solutions regarding the oil and gas production taken by the Romanian decision makers, in the 'Statoil' Company, exploiting the large oil deposits of Norwegian territorial waters, the Norwegian State has a majority stake of 67%. In addition, the Norwegian government -taking care of its own people- distributes some of the oil profits to the Norwegian citizens. Instead, by the fact that God gave the poor Romanians oil and gas, only the citizens of rich foreign countries (Austria, Canada, etc.) make a profit of those natural resources.

In Romania the control over the monopolies of

electricity distribution have been taken over by foreign companies, as follows. 'Electrica Oltenia' was privatized on 167 million euros in favor of Czech 'CEZ' Company (actually sold to the Czech State, since 69.78% of the shares of 'CEZ' belong to the Ministry of Finance of the Czech Republic). 'Electrica Moldova' company was sold to 'E. ON' Company in Dusseldorf with 100 million euros. 'Electrica Banat and Dobrogea' were sold with 112 million to Italian company 'Enel' (in which the main shareholder is the Ministry of Economy and Finance of Italy with a stake of 31.2%). In 2008, the Italian company 'Enel' bought for 820 million euros, 64.4% stake in 'Electrica Sud', the largest electricity distribution company in Romania. We gave the prices of 'privatization', to highlight the fact that Romania (an European country, the seventh largest in the European Union) finally gave foreigners the monopoly of electricity distribution for a sum of only 1.199 million euros! Foreign investors can recover the funds invested in just a few years, given the monopolist character of electricity distribution.

The wind energy sector in Romania was also transferred to foreigners. Thus, the investments in Dobrogea were made by Czech 'CEZ' Company, Italian 'Enel' Company, 'Energias de Portugal' Company (from Portugal) and 'Iberdrola Renovables' Company (from Spain). In 2011, in Romania 850 MW wind power was installed (ie, more power than a nuclear reactor in Cernavoda). In early 2012, there were over 1000 wind turbines that produce 3% of total energy in Romania.

We ask the question, why in France, Germany, Italy, Norway, Spain, Portugal, Czech Republic, etc., state-owned companies are efficient and compete successfully in the market economy? Could this really be because in those countries, they do not practice the 'flaying' of the national patrimony with the approval gotten from above? Unfortunately, it was wanted that the Romanian state to be a poor administrator, for the simple reason that all those who succeeded to get the power desired to be able to become rich beyond measure.

Professor Anghel N. Rugina said that the state monopoly is bad, but that the private monopoly is even worse. And when monopolies are transferred to foreign ownership, is a hundred times worse. He had the same opinion regarding the privatization and selling to foreigners of the mineral resources of the country. Today, the Romanian citizens are forced to buy in their own country, electricity, gas and water from foreign owners of these natural monopolies. Not being other suppliers, the Romanians are forced to buy regardless of what conditions and prices the foreign owners would impose. In reality, 'Petrom' and 'Romtelecom' are also, by their nature a kind of semi-monopolies. The same economist, with obstinately repeated that the economics must be taken into account together with the ecology and with the social factors. We would add that the national interest should be also taken into account.

How were taken into account in Romania all these precepts? As far as we know, in the world over there is no other country (even among the former colonies in Africa, Asia or Latin America) in which it was destroyed to such an extent almost all its industry and agriculture, in which the commercial fleet and the ocean fishing fleet have disappeared, or in which it was transferred to foreigners in such great proportions, the banks, the oil and gas resources, the monopolies of electricity, gas and water distributions, etc. The rulers of Romania have avoided to take the example from Putin's Russia, ie of using oil and gas (energy and strategic mineral deposits as well), as an important lever for promoting the national interest. They liked and like better, contrary to national interest, to give them all in the hands of the foreigners. For the Romanian rulers and policy-makers all that counts is to enrich themselves and their relatives and close associates. In Romania there is absolutely no way that politicians will become poor, in the period when they are in power. Instead, they continued and continue to get rich even when they are in the opposition.

Romania has the economic status of colony

At the present time, those in power, realizing that their mandate is coming to an end, endeavor in earnest to give foreigners control over what's left of the national heritage. We refer to gold and silver deposits and as well to the deposits of uranium, copper and rare metals (including wolfram and other elements of strategic importance), to thermoelectric and hydroelectric plants and the electro-nuclear plant in Cernavoda. If they will manage to "get rid of" all these, the future generations of citizens of Romania (an European country and a member of the European Union) no longer will own anything in their own country. They will be serving the foreign Companies or multinationals, as modern slaves. Each day that passes, more suitable become the words of the Romanian poet named Octavian Goga, in its volume titled "The songs of a Man with no Country", published in 1916: "Our mountains, golden fleet, we are begging on the street ..." Also, "With no Country" remained the generations both current and future! Unfortunately, the words "begging on the street" is actual too; just as the British press wrote about some Romanian citizens that: "They use children to beg on the streets of London."

Although in recent years, no other country has sold to foreigners its mineral resources, the current rulers of Romania decided in March 2012 to sell the 'Cupru Min Abrud' Company -the owner of 'Rosia Poieni' Mines- to the Canadian company 'Roman Copper Corporation'. The tender was won by the Canadian company, in exchange for 200.8 million euros (U.S. $ 267 million). The deposits of 'Rosia Poieni' Mines, located 6 km from 'Rosia Montana' Mines, holds proven reserves of one million tons of copper (and probable reserves of 50 million!). Here are 60% of the copper deposits of Romania, placed second in Europe after those of Russia (whose reserves are actually in Siberia).

Strangely, the Romanian rulers have decided to sell both mines 'Rosia Poieni' and 'Rosia Montana', in conditions as if they were physically removed from Romania (a poor country), to a super-rich country (Canada). The stipulated royalty (6%) -until thorough depletion of deposits- is completely negligible! This time, the excuse often used, that Romania was forced by the European Union to accept this "business" is not valid; as far as we know, Canada is not a member state of the Union! A protester, that used to work in 'Rosia Poieni' Mines, had the courage (very rare in Romania) to ask the minister: "How much bribe (kickback) you got?"

It seems that are pure illusions of all those who hope that, if the current governing will lose power, those who will take over the affairs of the country will do otherwise for all these key issues for the future of Romanians. The opposition parties only in words are different from those currently in power; their interests and morals are identical. So that, if the opposition comes to power, in all probability, the plunder and the selling cheep to foreigners of what remains of the national patrimony, will continue. Woe and alas for the poor Romanians!

In terms of ownership structure of the national wealth and economy, Romania finds itself in a worse state than before world war two. Actually today, Romania has the economic status of colony, a status that is not allowed anymore even by Latin American countries. This fact is deduced if the financial flows into and out of Romania are examined.

Serious is also the fact that the money resulting from the numerous privatizations and concessions of the national heritage and resources (all underestimated), simply disappeared like water in the desert. As a follow up, did not result in significant investments in infrastructure or in new industries. Exactly the same fate had circa 100 billion euros that Romania owes abroad. In 1990, Romania had no foreign debt! A lot of the current today debts belong to the Romanian state. So the question is how will be managed their repayment, taking into account that the state budget sources are exclusively of fiscal nature, that is from taxes. Its economy has been substantially diminished and almost all the profits of the part of economy that has survived belong to their new foreign owners. Moreover, a renowned economist said on television that, every year, about 50 billion euros are getting out of Romania; the amount is excessive if reported to the GDP of 136.4 billion euros achieved in 2011. In the 50 billion are included: the amount to cover the trade deficit, the dues to the European Union budget, the interest and repayment rates on foreign loans and the profits of the foreigners that own most of the Romanian economy (here, are enclosed also the earnings -illicit in their substance- resulting in overpriced imports and exports at reduced prices).

Even if Romania would fully use the approximately 34.7 billion euros provided as European funds for seven years (which is completely unlikely given the low rate of accessing), the nearly 5 billion per year is only a tiny part of the funds mentioned above that flow out of the country per year. In other words, although Romania is a member of the European Union, it is 'de facto' treated as the former colonies in Africa. Ie, cash flows coming out of the country are actually much larger than financial aid received.

In a TV show dated December 28, 2011, the sources of the Romanian state budget for 2011 were presented. Of total receipts of 44 billion euros, was expected to be collected from consumers 15.75 billion euros in the form of excise duties and VAT. Receipts of 14.25 billion euros ware provided, also from the entire population, as an income tax on individuals and as social security and health taxes. These receipts (the same percentage for the poor or rich) totaled 30 billion euros or 68.2% of total expected income. As tax on profits were stipulated 2.5 billion euros, i.e. a percentage of 5.7% of the budget. Effective tax on profits charged in 2010, was even smaller, namely 1.8 billion euros. The same TV channel mentioned, several times, that the foreign investors in Romania (including the large ones) arrange their accounts so as to emerge with minimal profits or just losses. Consequently, they manage to evade the payment of a substantial tax on profits.

From the above figures one can see that the Romanian state budget burden hangs, largely on the common people. The enormous profits that are obtained actually in the natural monopolies in

Romania, go to the foreign state budgets, as follows. Much of the profits from 'Distrigaz Sud' (owned by 'GDF Suez') fuel the budget of France. In the same way, much of the profits from the power distributions 'Electrica Banat and Dobrogea', 'Electrica Sud' and Dobrogea windmill installations, controlled by 'Enel', are source of Italy's budget; those of 'Electrica Oltenia' and of other windmill installations of Dobrogea controlled by 'CEZ', represent a source for the Czech budget. The bulk of the profits, which covered several times the price of "privatization" of 'Petrom', is fueling the budgets of Austria and of Abu Dhabi. Following the "privatization", the profits of 'Rompetrol' became entirely a source to the state budget of the former Soviet Republics of Kazakhstan! On the last hundred meters, the current rulers of Romania make all endeavors that the famous 'Rosia Montana' and 'Rosia Poieni' mines, with their huge mineral deposits, enrich the wealthy Canadians. Similar endeavors are made, relating to exploitation by the foreigners of the gas shale deposits. Some time ago, rulers of Romania boasted that, at the international courts, have obtained the oil and gas perimeters in the vicinity of 'Snake Island' in Black Sea. But they forgot to mention that, years ago, those oil and gas perimeters were already leased "disinterestedly" (with the approval of former prime ministers) to foreign companies.

To underline the seriousness of the situation in which Romania is today, let assume that God would take the minds of all American politicians and would do what the Romanian political class has already done, namely: would sell to the foreign countries all American oil and gas reserves together with Exxon Mobil, Chevron, Texaco and the other oil companies; would sell to the foreign countries all American banks (JP Morgan Chase Bank, Bank of America, Citibank, etc.); would sell to foreign companies the monopolies of electricity, gas and water distributions; would pass a law similar to the Romanian Law No. 10/2001, which would return to the Native Americans all that has belonged to them before the arrival of the first settlers in America with the 'Mayflower' boat; would spray the American agricultural land in plots of under one hectare; would cut the superb American forests and would export them as logs; would dispel the American merchant and fishing fleets; would destroy the research and development departments of Microsoft, Lockheed Martin etc.. If all these would happen, the United States would not only lose superpower status, but would be in danger of disappearing as a state and as a country.

Some argue that because of the globalization, the manufacturing industries have disappeared in other countries, not only in Romania. Indeed, today in the American malls we can not find garments, knitwear and jeans or even computers with labels 'Made in USA'. All are 'Made in China', 'Made in India', 'Made in Honduras, etc. However, because of cost considerations, their manufacturing was only transferred to countries where wages are much lower. But usually, the companies that are producing those goods are U.S. property. Conception, research and development, design and production management are all American. Obviously, the largest part of the profit obtained is also American. So, the manufacturing was only transferred, while in Romania it was disbanded or simply liquidated. Romanian investments abroad are virtually zero. Instead, smaller nations, including countries that belonged to Eastern bloc as the Czech Republic, Hungary and Kazakhstan, have now major investments in Romania.

The American literature rightly says that globalization is Westernization. We would add that globalization is actually Americanization; the Americans had introduced all over the globe not only goods originally developed in the United States but also products and concepts such as Windows, Laptops & Notebooks, GPS, Youtube, Twitter, Facebook, iPhone, Yahoo, Google, Skype, Space Shuttle, Coca-cola, KFC, McDonald's, Xerox, etc. Equally true is that, as far as it seems, from this globalization have benefited especially the emerging countries, namely China (which has become the world's largest manufacturer and second world economic power), India, Brazil etc. Although the American owners who transferred their manufacturing to foreign countries get fat profits (otherwise would not have wanted such a transfer), ordinary Americans are, every day, becoming less enjoied and think that the lack of jobs in their home country is due to globalization.

Crisis causes are internal in origin, but there were also external influences

The Romanians have a distinguished history that goes back to the Roman emperor Trajan, whose legions defeated the army of the king Decebal of Dacia in 106 a.d. After the Romanian principalities Moldavia and Wallachia escaped, in the 14th century, from the suzerainity of the Hungarian kings, they had to carry heavy fighting against the Ottoman Turks, who conquered the Bizantin Empire and finaly Constantinople in 1453. With the Turkish Ottoman Empire on the south, the Habsburg empire (called the dual Austro-Hungarian Empire later) on the west and the Russian Empire on the east, at the beginning of the sixteenth century, the territories inhabited by the Romanians were entirely under their domination. In addition, most of the wars these great empires fought between themselves took place on Romanian territory. So, the Romanians passed through nearly four centuries of sufferings "endured in a Christian way", as stated on the Triumphal Arch in Bucharest. After Romanian principalities Moldavia and Wallachia were united in 1859 under a common ruler, that of Prince Alexandru Ioan Cuza, it began a process of modernization. In 1877, the 'United Principalities' have gained independence from the Turkish-Ottoman 'High Gate' in Istanbul, later taking the name of Romania. On 1 December 1918, the union of Transylvania with Romania took place as well.

Because of a troubled history and of the negative

and retrograde influences of the foreign occupations, especially of the Turkish-Ottoman one, the Romanians were living, at all times, much harder than the other European nations. For the same reasons, from the early times until nowadays, those who were in the leadership of the country have entered politics to enrich themselves, and not for the national interest.

The current situation of the country is due largely to the voluntarism and incompetence of the political-administrative and economic leaders of the communist dictatorship (especially those from the period 1980-1989 of Ceausescu). However, despite the strong downturn that occurred in the last decade of the Communist rule, at that time Romania was producing and exporting from needles to combat aircraft, and there were cost-effective external relationships with over a hundred countries. There was also an effective education system, a satisfying social protection and a moral population, educated in the cult of labor and honor. December 1989 found Romania with no external debt and with cash reserves of 4.5 billion dollars, 1.6 billion transferable rubles and hundreds of billions of strong Romanian 'lei', gathered in special funds (of the former political and social organizations, of the military, of the interior ministry and of other ministries, etc.)

Also, the Romanian economy was found in full operation, with more than 70% of factories and works upgraded, with more than one million specialists with higher education and post-secondary training, with an efficient procurement and export system, with a large number of people directly involved in the productive sphere and a small number of retired persons.

After December 1989, the political-administrative and economic leaders, and the religious leaders as well, destroyed a large part of the Romanian economy, from the part that remained they have sold cheap the most profitable industries and economic objectives, they proletarianized all Romanian population that used to own the national wealth, reduced drastically the national ownership in favor of foreign companies, the number of direct creators was lowered severely, while the volume of inactive population rose; the Romanian state was led to a position of a bankrupted semi-colony.

Shaken by the scale of the destruction, the other day, a TV viewer suggested that the walls and ruins of the former factories and plants, breeding compexes, etc., are not to be removed completely. Together with the Dacian and Roman-era ruins or the medieval ruins, the ruins of the former Romanian economy has to be preserved so that the future generations could see how many factories and plants had Romania before December 1989.

Immediately after December 1989, it would had been normal to proceed urgently to fructify the resources available to Romania at that time (industry and agriculture in which enormous financial funds had been invested, well qualified human resources, greater natural resources than those existing in the neighboring countries and plus a zero external debt). Instead, said Professor Anghel N. Rugina, those who got the power came with an "anti-national argument that all industry built by hard work of the (Romanian) people would have no value and that everything should be restructured along the lines of the Western economy." The country's Premier in those days said, no more no less, that the Romanian industry "is a pile of scrap iron!" The process of decomposition of the national economy was triggered. Professor Anghel N. Rugina states that " the advice and solutions given by the foreign experts have been blindly accepted by the Romanian experts. In this way, inevitably they came to conditions requiring foreign credits and loans from IMF, World Bank and (from) other financial institutions in the West." Professor Rugina also stated that in the Romanian economy, over the imbalances inherited from the communist period "it was grafted a second wave of imbalance imported from the West by imitating Western capitalist system which has its contradictions also."

Currently, all the guilty persons, for the desperate position of Romania, want to come out of the current crisis by the sacrifices of the masses of children, students, budget personnel, retired persons and small entrepreneurs. In compensation, their political-economic and religious clienteles will stuff themselves on the work and sacrifices of ordinary Romanians.

The income reduction of the budget personnel by 25% and by 5.5% of a part of the retired persons, is causing large-scale genocide, by starvation, malnutrition, lack of medical assistance, lack of facilities of a modern living (gas, hot and cold water, electricity, telephone, etc.), to millions of Romanian citizens, that are already at the lower limit of endurance. As a general rule, every citizen active or retired requires at least 1,000 Romanian 'lei' (229 euros) per month to survive. Nobody has the right to lower the income of the citizens under this limit, except in duly justified cases such as in alcoholics, lazy, those who refused or refuse to work etc.

One can see already that the program imposed by the IMF and accepted by the Government, after contracting, on May 4, 2009, the loan of 20 billion euros, has not led to the improvement of the difficult situation of Romania. Conversely, there are signs that the situation will worsen further if the said program will continue to apply. It is therefore necessary for the Government to find other sources to exit the current crisis. In this essay we will propose such alternatives.

The main reasons for which Romania has reached the current situation, of course, is internal. Overwhelmingly the responsibility belongs to all rulers, governments and decision makers that came to power after December 1989, most of them disconnected from the Romanian people and its legitimate interests.

But we don't have to forget the external influences. Two former "communist" countries, Yugoslavia and Romania, directly or indirectly, had supported the West and United States especially, in some of the most difficult phases of the long Cold War. The role of Romania is now well known and results from the publication, on the Internet, of transcripts of the conversations of Ceausescu with Nixon and Kisinger and is also revealed in the statements made on the television, in 2011, by an U.S. citizen named Larry Watts. He published a book on the subject, based on data from official archives, as well.

Paradoxically, after the collapse of the eastern bloc, Yugoslavia and Romania were most severely punished. Yugoslavia was dismantled and some of it bombed. Romania escaped with less harm; only its economy was destroyed! As we have shown, so great losses and damages did not occur not even during the world war two, although the German-Soviet front line crossed the entire Romanian territory from east to west. It seems that the cold war had more dreadful consequences for Romania than the terrible world war two. That, though over the years, Romania has played a dual role, actually supporting occasionally the Soviet bloc, occasionally the United States. Is it maybe exactly for this reason, that Romania got such a treatment?

Since the world war two, the Romanians still hoped that "the Americans were coming". So, after the Revolution of 1989 they were expecting the US and the West to show their gratitude for the support received from Romania in some actions as were: the US-Chinese rapprochement, ending the Vietnam War and the reconciliation attempts of Israel with the Arabic countries. Romania was the first Eastern bloc country that established diplomatic relations with the FRG and did not brake relations with Israel when Moscow asked it. All these were forgotten, and Romania came to be regarded today as a kind of black sheep of the European Union. It seems that there is no thankful appreciation among countries, but only interests.

It's hard to explain and even more to accept the current deindustrialization and of the cheap selling to foreigners of what remained of the Romanian economy. In the past, even the much blamed Soviet Union did not actually apply such a policy in Romania. It was the other way around; during the time of 'Sovrom', new industries were founded.

The 'Sovrom' were Soviet-Romanian joint venture companies established in 1945, following an agreement between Romania and the Soviet Union signed on May 8, 1945. The Soviet side participation in their social capital was constituted partly with the confiscated German properties in Romania and partly with money from the obligations of Romania for war damages against the Soviet Union. In accordance with the ceasefire agreement (September 1944) and the Paris Peace Treaties (1947), Romania has been imposed damages of $ 300 million, at their 1938 value.

During the 'Sovrom' times, the new industries were created by expanding and changing the production profile of existing companies. For example, during world war two, 'Concordia' Company in Ploiesti produced, together with the Germans, 'Schneider' anti-tank guns and containers for tanker-trucks. In 1945, the

'Concordia' Company were enclosed in the 'Sovrom' for oilfield equipment, changing its name to '1 Mai' Ploiesti Company (then 'Upetrom 1 Mai'). In the management of the company only the chief engineer was Romanian; the general manager and technical manager were Soviet citizens. The first oil drilling rigs (which subsequently became one of Romania's successfully exported equipment) were produced with the documentation that came from the Soviet Union. In fact, the Soviet technical drawings were translated into the Romanian language, and the Russian "Uralmaş Zavod" replaced with the name of the Romanian Company.

Between 1945 - 1950, the 'IMS Campulung Muscel' Company (then 'ARO'), repaired the vehicles of the Romanian and Soviet armies. The first off-road vehicles produced, were inspired from the Soviet 'GAZ' cars. The 'ARO' Company produced, until its privatization and bankruptcy, over 380,000 vehicles, of which two thirds were exported to over 110 countries. The first Romanian trucks ('Steagul Rosu') produced in Brasov were inspired by Soviet ZIS trucks.

Of course there were many negative aspects of the 'Sovrom'; by that reason the Romanian side endeavored to dismantle them. It is enough to remember the case of 'Sovromcuarţit' Company, set up in December 31, 1951, which dealt with the extraction of uranium from Stei and Baita Mines. From these mines was extracted the ore with the highest concentration of uranium in the world. 'Sovromcuarţit' and 'Sovrompetrol', the last two 'Sovrom' companies were dissolved in October 22, 1956, when the Convention of taking over by the Romanian side was signed. During the existence 'Sovromcuarțit' Company, and four years after its cancellation, the Stei and Baita Mines delivered to the Soviet Union about 18,000 tons of uranium metal, under net unfavorable conditions for the Romanian state.

Got under the guardianship of the democratic West, Romania did not expect that many of its industries (including those whose foundations were laid in the days of the 'Sovrom' companies) would be knocked down. Because of the deindustrialization of Romania, now this country has to import even wheelbarrows (from Italy) and cotton thread for sewing machines (from Hungary). Romanian cotton spinning companies have been dismantled, including those established before the First World War.

The best graduates of the Romanian schools, in the benefice of the rich countries

In early July 2011, the press and television debated extensively the disastrous results obtained by the students at the high school graduation exams, respectively at the baccalaureate. Failure in these tests was over 50%.

Ordinarily, in a normal country, the quality of education at all its levels, is very important. But paradoxically, after 1989 has resulted that it is not at all in the benefice of Romania to produce well trained graduates. This is simply because the vast majority of them prefer to leave Romamia and to work abroad permanently. The better prepared are the youngsters by the Romanian school, more of them leave for the world over, thus damaging the country which spent so much for their cultural and professional training. Almost all Romanians who took prizes at international Olympiads (in Mathematics, Physics, Chemistry etc) have emigrated. An another concrete and sad example to mention is the fact that, absolutely all the graduates of a certain year in Electronics from the Polytechnic Institute of Bucharest, have emigrated.

The academics and the faculty say that most of their students have only one thought, namely how to leave Romania as soon as posible. Millions of people left and are still leaving, especially those considered to be able to compete in the West (tougher competition than in Romania). Thousands of doctors had left. After, the poorest country in the European Union spends seriously on their training (6 years of university plus several years of residency), they finally heal patients in rich countries like England, Canada, France, etc. The same considerations are valid for computer programmers who are working at Microsoft Company in the U.S. (there, it is said that the Romanian language became the second most spoken language after English). The Romanian rulers are encouraging these departures, they don't realize that the immigration of the specialists (the "brain drain") is not only a huge loss for the country but also a tragedy! The media say that abroad are working between 3.6 and 4 million Romanian citizens (no one knows their exact number).

The consequences of neoliberalism

In the following, we will present briefly the actual consequences of the politics and of the measures applied in Romania after December 1989 (of course, all of them were consistent with the principles of contemporary neoliberalism).

By examining the situation of different countries around the world, you can notice that the application of neoliberalism has given certain results in the former colonial powers, and completely different in the former colonies. Consequences of neoliberalism in poor countries were generally negative for most of the populations. Up through 2007 (the year when the new global financial and economic crisis started), the neoliberalism has given very positive results in the rich countries. The results of neoliberalism, during 20-22 years, in the former "communist" countries were disappointing for the most of the people, and very gratifying for a tiny strata of the freshly enriched people ('les nouveaux riches'). In this category of countries, the most disastrous results were obtained in Romania. This can be proved by figures.

In 1989 the number of employees in Romania was 7.997 million, of which 3.799 million in industry, 717,400 in construction, 601,600 in agriculture, 364,200 in education, culture, art and 159 100 in science, research and development. To show that it was not only the quantity but also a highly qualified staff, we will give some examples that speak for themselves.

In an instance, we were convinced by the aviation traditions of Romania, after long discussions with an engineer who developed the famous "IS" gliders and moto-gliders. After 1957 Romania became the main exporter of such aircraft in the world. Most were exported to the West.

Often in difficult conditions, in the forced industrialization of Romania in the aftermath of World War Two, Romanian experts and workers have designed, built and installed modern plants, in which were produced machine tools, transportation and power equipments, electronics, automation, computers, telecommunication and military equipments, cathode ray tubes, medicines, and many other products. They also built cement factories, petrochemical complexes, refineries, fertilizer plants, high voltage power lines and poultry complexes, not only in Romania but also in the Middle East and North Africa. They did prospecting and oil wells were drilled in the USSR and in North Africa. Romania has built a refrigerators factory in China, energy groups in Turkey and the Philippines etc. Machine tools were exported even to the U.S. ('General Electric' CNC were mounted on them). From talks with foreign customers has resulted that the Romanian staff successfully won some competitions, even if sometimes it came from advanced countries. The specialists in agriculture have created, both within Romania and in

Africa, new varieties of plants and livestock. Romanian experts and workers have built modern hydropower plants. They built the Bucharest underground metro, the Danube-Black Sea canal and the irrigations on 3 million hectares. They drained and regulated the river Dambovita. It was built and designed, with personnel and materials exclusively from Romania, the largest palace in the world (the former 'People's House' that became the 'Palace of Parliament'). After December 89, Romania may pride that mainly villas and buildings (some monumental) were built for the freshly enriched people.

Most manufacturing belong to the past. A lot of manufacturing licenses and trademarks purchased from leading foreign companies, with huge amount of free currency, today are good for nothing; their manufacturing objects disappeared along with the respective plants, works and factories.

Unfortunately, after December 1989, in Romania the situation regarding the employed personnel (including trained personnel), instead of improving, deteriorated badly. According to data of the 'National Statistics Institute', the number of employees in Romania has dropped to 4.57 million at the end of October 2010. Due to lack of jobs, millions of fellow citizens, among the most well trained and able to work, had to go to foreign countries to earn their living. In the entire two thousand years history, the Romanian people has never had such an exodus of population. Neither in the time of the barbarian invasions! Curiously, this serious phenomenon leaves the Romanian rulers and politicians completely indifferent.

In the country remained only the elders, the less competitive people and those who could get good jobs at home, on their relations with those in power.

In 1989 Romania's population was 23,151,564 inhabitants. The provisional data of the 2011 census, shows that the stable population in Romania was at that time, of 19,042,936 inhabitants. The lack of 4,108,628 inhabitants consists of those who left to foreign countries and due to the natural diminution of population.

With a population of 501,062,000 in 2010, the European Union has 221 368 000 employees; ie a percentage of 44.18%. At such a percentage, at the current population, Romania should have 8.42 million employees, which is nearly twice the number of employees existing now. The current number of employees, at the existent EU percentage of employees in relation to the population, Romania's population should be no more than 10,335,653 inhabitants. The figure is actually the maximum population that can sustained by the current number of employees in Romania! This figure alone is more than enough to demonstrate the disaster reached in Romania.

It is known that the number of jobs in the economy of a country has influence on the size of GDP per capita and on the standard of living. In Romania, there was a drastic reduction in the number of employees. The decrease was not only a quantitative one but also qualitative, due to the fact that, as already shown, those who left to earn a piece of bread in foreign countries, were those most able to work.

It should be shown that prior to December 1989, the Romanians were proud to be a nation of turners, milling cutters, locksmiths, welders, steelworkers, carpenters, miners, tractor drivers, agricultural machine operators, caretakers of livestock, horticulturalists and so on. In Romania, many thousands of sailors worked, one of them even became president of Romania. Today, after dismantling of the commercial fleet and of the ocean fishing fleet, one can hear about a Romanian sailor when some foreign ship is captured by Somali pirates.

After December 1989, as expected, the largest reduction in the number of employees in Romania took place in industry and research - development. Drastic cuts have occurred among all types of engineers and technical experts, including agronomists. Lower number exists or even disappeared in some of the following occupations: turner, milling cutters, locksmith, welder, coppersmith, blacksmith, steel worker, sailor, carpenter, miner, agricultural mechanic and caretakers of livestock. In exchange, Romania became a country of bodyguards, you can see them everywhere. On the Internet it was stated (based on foreign sources) that Romania became the largest exporter of prostitutes, beggars and pickpockets in the European Union (the total number of them reach nearly 1 million!). Even if this figure is greatly exaggerated, unfortunately it reflects the perception of foreigners and shows the degree of economical and social decay of Romania.

In December 1989 almost all Romanians believed that if Romania will have the same regime like that existing in the West (multi-party system, freedom of speech, free elections, etc.), automatically they will live as the Westerners. After the Revolution were created dozens of parties. Everyone is talking now freely (some of them even curse the rulers and the governments!). Elections are becoming free. Romanians are free to vote as they like. The poorest people have even the right to sell their vote for 20 euros, or a bag of food!

Unfortunately, the standard of living depends not only on the freedoms which the Romanians actually have won. So far, despite the fact that Romania had richer natural resources than the surrounding countries and had liquidated its foreign debt before 1989, the Romanians' living standard is considered the lowest in the European Union. To see the huge disparity with other countries, we will give the values of minimum wages in Romania and in several EU countries. In Romania the current minimum wage is 162 euros per month. In Hungary (though that country has nowhere near the resources existing in Romania) is of 297 euros. In Italy, 750 euros. In Greece, 877 euros. In Germany, 1200 euro. In France, 1398 euros.

To make a long story short, we will state that there are about the same differences in terms of average salary and pension. At the end of 2011 the average net salary in Romania was 325 euros and the average pension was 173 euros. Despite differences in wages, prices of petrol and basic foodstuffs in Romania are close to those of the countries mentioned. On some products, prices are even higher in Romania than in some of the countries to which the comparison was made. For these reasons, there are enormous differences between the standard of living of most EU countries, compared with Romania. However, in 2010, various bonuses of the budgeteers were eliminated, while their salaries were reduced by 25%. From

January 1, 2011 the pensions have been reduced, since those with monthly income of more than 740 RON (170 euros) had to pay a health fee of 5.5%.

Only in the first months of 2012, government officials discussed about returning to the old nominal wages. Even if this will be done, the purchasing power of those wages would be lower, given the abrupt rise in prices in recent two years.

The mentioned statistical average figures do not reveal the entire drama of the the poor people in Romania. This is because in no other country in the European Union, there is such a huge gap between the low wages and the high revenues existing in Romania. However, the current 'anti-crisis measures' adopted in this country, affects only those in the lower strata of the population. Explanation of this situation lies in the fact that the fate of politicians and of the top rulers do not depend at all of how the people get through to survive;

they are completely decoupled from the general course. The country can go bankrupted, they all are doing increasingly better!

After December 1989 unemployment in Romania emerged as one of the negative phenomena of our times, the leading cause of this being the deindustrialization and job losses caused by it. Without industry, the prosperity for the whole population can not be achieved. Of course, the situation before 1990, when a job allocation was provided by law for each citizen fit to work, was not rational neither. This measure was anti-economic and led to the inefficiencies in those days.

Negative is also the penetration the ethno-botanical substances and of the drugs, including in schools. The illiteracy reappeared. At EU level, Romania has the highest percentage of young people with difficulty of reading a written text.

The patriotic feeling has diminished visibly. Youth does not believe anymore in the ancient Romanian saying which said; "even with a poor bread, is much better in your own country." Now is fashionable the ancient Latin saying: "ubi bene, ibi patria". So, millions of Romanians have left their country, settling all over the world. Many of them came not only to Europe but to USA, Canada, Australia, Latin America and Japan as well. The truth forces us to mention that the prestige and fame of the Romanians abroad were seriously deteriorated. Because of improper behavior of some (and probably due to poverty), the Romanians are now considered almost undesirable in Italy and even in Spain.

The foreigners who visit Romania can notice the disappointment, resignation, skepticism, frustration and hopelessness of the people. The Romanians are a tired people, they don't have energy and will anymore to fight for their rights. They are discouraged especially by the generalized corruption and by the reversed value chain. Since, in the leadership of the country some semi-illiterate people had perched, ordinary people conclude that they can do nothing. They tell themselves: "how to make things better, when we have mayors, ministers and representatives -including in the European Parliament- who have knowledge and express themselves like ones who did not finish a primary school?!"

Bucharest, like many other major cities in Romania, offer increasingly difficult housing and living conditions. This is both because of pollution, as well as due to the fact that the car became powerful and pervasive. Some American visitors said, in 1968, that unlike in their U.S. cities, in Bucharest was nice to walk about, both during the day and the night. They appreciated and praised the existing vegetation everywhere ("the tree-lined streets"). Unfortunately today the situation is completely changed. After December 1989, in the capital city of Romania a million trees were cut down, and two other million in the woods around Bucharest. They say that, less than 25% of the trees existing in 1989 remained today. In

Bucharest is not pleasing to walk anymore. On 'Victoriei' Avenue and on other streets in downtown, you no longer can see people walking. There are no pedestrians even on the 'Sosea', a promenade avenue in the old times. On all streets and boulevards it is a continuous traffic of cars. Bucharest is not a city of people anymore; today it is mastered by the automotive.

Romanians are increasingly disconnected from nature. Lyrics like "The Romanians love to live / Up in the mountains / Where the springs of the brook are", belong to the past. The climbing of the mountains and walking through the woods are no longer practiced on mass scale, as in the past. When the Romanians have to move along a few hundred meters, they go by car, by bus or by streetcar. They go increasingly less and less to the theater and read less books. The television made them sedentary. They are increasingly stressed by the flood of information and of news (most of them being negative). The nerves are overloaded by the rapid changes.

In Romania, the gap between rich and poor is greater than in rich countries

In the old times, all revolutions (the American Revolution between 1763 and 1791, the French Revolution that began in 1789, the European revolutions of 1848, the Zapata and Pancho Villa's revolution in Mexico, the Russian revolutions - those of

February and October 1917, etc.) actually reduced the gap between rich and poor. Precisely the opposite happened after the Romanian Revolution of 1989 and after the revolutionary events of the period 1989-1991, that overthrew the "communist" regimes in Eastern Europe. In reality, the polarization of society reached is so pronounced, that it is unusual even in countries where the capitalism system had endured for centuries. Those who have grabbed fabulous wealth overnight, are called "oligarchs" in the former USSR (the so called "country of victorious socialism"), and "moguls" in Romania. In the U.S., a Bill Gates became one of the richest people on earth on personal merits; the 'Windows' created by him had not only a commercial success, but revolutionized the lives of all people in the world. The enrichment methods practiced in the former eastern bloc countries were different from country to country, but they had a common denominator, namely that some people chosen by fate (and by those who grabbed the power) became the owners of state properties of the former "communist" countries. As a rule, the newly enriched people did not invented any products or technologies, but simply they took over the role as owners of the national economy, a role belonging before to the state.

Openly or underground and behind the scenes, the newly enriched ('les nouveaux riches') are hand in hand with politicians, especially with those in power. The media in Romania has discussed, until saturation, about laws passed "with dedication" in favor of some, about bid rigging, about marble deposits, mineral water springs or city pavement for parking spaces, all granted to "darlings or sweethearts", etc. The greed of the newly enriched people in Romania exceeds that of Balzac's characters. Former nomenclaturists of yesterday were transformed into the capitalists and the politicians of today. From truly convinced atheists, they even became humble Christians before the altars, as if had not never been part of the communist nomenclature. On TV we could see that, two prime ministers (one married to a wife from the nomenclature and the other a son of an NKDV general) and a President (former Propaganda Secretary of the Romanian Communist Party during Ceausescu) were competing with each other, how to do the largest and most spectacular sign of cross.

The morality and the humbleness are faked more openly, as they climb up the ladder of power and wealth. In fact, they do not sincerely believe in the Gospel precepts! In the quotations used by us as "Moto" of this essay, even less! They believe only in money and they worship it. It seems that nowadays this is common for rich countries and for the poor Romania too.

It is known that the one of the main causes for the collapse of former Eastern bloc regimes was that, lying deeply penetrated all levels of society and especially in economics. Unfortunately the lie, this anti-economical sin proliferate to this day. When the Romanian politicians are in opposition, they reveal some negative aspects of the economy; of course, not the essential ones and in no way those due to them.

Once they grab the power the politicians start to tell a lot of lies, their only concern is to get rich. Certainly they did not strive so hard to

be elected for the "benefice" of the voters! When they are in power, suddenly, the economic reality is beginning to be described by them in pink shades; the politics and measures dictated by them are considered not only necessary but the only ones possible. And they do have "a wonderful life" spending Romania's money, until the next elections will take place over four or six years. And may, part of the media (the one that was not bought with money from the budget) and the people criticize and grumble endlessly, that those who grabbed the power don't give a damn. In Romania, there is freedom of speech in the sense that anyone can say anything. Only, the impact of his words depends on access to newspapers, television, etc. But these means are all either under political control or conditioned by the commercial interest of the owners. The common man does not have access to them.

An ancient proverb reads: "dog does not eat dog." The wealthy people and the politicians (especially when in power) have identical goals and interests. The lower strata of population, ie the vast majority of Romania's population, have no power and no money. Nobody ask their opinion on matters essential to their livelihood. For example, the Romanian people were not asked if they agree or disagree with selling cheep the Romanian banks, the gold, oil and gas deposits, etc. Instead, they were asked in a referendum if they agree with an unicameral parliament, although such a change will not be a substantial one; anyhow in this way will not improve the life of Romanians. The common people do not have sufficient expertise and real information. They can be easily manipulated.

What to do?

In the above we summarized the problems facing contemporary society in Romania. At the country level we ask, what to do? Simple distribution of money (collected by taxation or borrowed, largely from abroad) and throwing the burden solely on the backs of the low strata of the population will not improve the situation in Romania. If the flat tax will be maintained, if all kinds of thefts, robbery and corruption will go on, if the state will not recover the natural monopolies and the mineral resources (those sold cheep to foreigners and given for almost nothing to native proteges), if there will be no suitable legislations against 'flaying' the national patrimony similar to that of Germany, France and Italy and if will not be adopted a fiscal and tax system like that existing in the U.S., if restitution will not have limited value as in neighboring countries, if the illicit assets will not be severely taxed or will not be recovered (including those captured with 'law in hand' or by the corruption of justice), then in the next few years other millions of competitive Romanians will choose the emigration solution. Those who decide the future of this country may not realize it, but from such a sequence would result, in the next 15 to 20 years, another Romania, in which the Romanians would become a minority. That, in addition to the fact, the country will become so poor that will not have enough money to pay its pensioners.

We believe that there can not be a competitive market economy without a domestic market to absorb a large part of production of goods and services. Therefore it is necessary to stimulate domestic demand, especially of the population which consume services and products produced in the country. We know that newly enriched people use limousines, house and office furniture, clothes and food imported from abroad and they spend their holidays on the Riviera, the Caribbean, etc. So, the earnings of the low-income and middle-income population should have a steep growth, thus expanding the market for domestically produced goods and a services.

In order that the state budget not be limited exclusively to tax sources, is necessary for the state to invest in sectors with high profitability potential. We refer to the gold, silver, uranium and rare metals mining, to the exploitation of oil and gas deposits from land and sea, of the marble and of the mineral and thermal waters. Since foreign banks, really, are not directly interested in the development of Romania, it is necessary for the state to invest heavily in the banking system, in this way will have appropriate economic levers as the needs continually change. Given the current conditions of global financial turbulence, states that give foreigners (and even to the natives) the control of the banking capital of the country, are committing a true economic suicide. Infrastructure investments should focus on motorways constructions. The waste of financial funds on ski gondolas in areas where there is little snow, on parks and swimming pools in villages, should be prohibited. For those villagers would be more useful if it would regulate and clean up the rivers, as they flood regularly and have reached a high degree of pollution.

To increase the standard of living of the entire population, Romania should be industrialized again until it reaches above the level existing in 1989. By keeping the current structure of the economy in Romania (as sectors, as well as types of property ownership), not only the current generation but also future ones are condemned to a terrible poverty.

We consider that Romania can get away from the current situation only by radical measures. Of course, comprehensive solutions we can not propose. They may follow only from a broad public debate on the situation in Romania from which a diagnosis, as realistic as possible, would result. However, we believe that the following brief course of radical actions would be beneficial for Romania.

a) To re-introduce a progressive income tax, giving up the current flat tax of 16%. Individuals with incomes up to the limit of subsistence (1,000 RON, about 228 euros / month) to be exempt from tax. Income from any source, between 1000 and 2000 RON / month to be taxed at 5%, etc. Revenues reaching more than 1,000,000 RON / month to be taxed at 75%;

b) To adopt and enforce a law of progressive taxation of all estates and properties, over 500,000 euros;

c) To adopt and enforce a law for the control of the origin of wealth, and the one that was not acquired lawfully to be seized by the state;

d) To adopt and enforce a legislation against tax evasion similar to that existing in the U.S.;

e) To renationalize all mineral resources (oil, gas, gold, silver, rare metals, marble, thermal and mineral water, etc.) and to prohibit their concession;

f) The State should become a major investor in companies in the extraction and exploitation of mineral resources (oil, gas, gold, silver, rare metals, marble, mineral and thermal waters etc.)

h) Since by their specificity can not ensure a competition, the natural monopolies (electricity, gas, water distributions, etc.) to be renationalized;

i) To forbid by law the privatization of the thermal, hydro and nuclear power plants, high voltage lines and the selling of electricity through intermediaries;

j) To amend the existing restitution legislation, ie to limit their restitution value to the level existing in neighboring countries;

k) To adopt and enforce a strict legislation against corruption and 'flaying' of public and state companies, similar to those existing in Germany, France and Italy;

l) With funding from the National Bank of Romania (BNR), to increase the social capital of CEC Bank, in order to become the largest commercial bank in the country. To prohibit by law the privatization of CEC Bank;

m) With the same funding from BNR, to reestablish the Agricultural Bank intended to finance the development of agriculture;

n) The state to become an major investor in banks, mutual funds and insurance companies;

o) To adopt and enforce a law of ministerial responsibility, including the provision that at the change of a government, to give and to receive the management of the country by drawing up a detailed official record. The same provisions, for the case when ministers change. The records will be approved by Parliament, and then made available to the public. The fraudulent management of the country or the serious damages to national heritage to be severely punished.

We realize that in order to adopt the above measures, it would be necessary to produce major changes in the current legislation. In this respect there should be political will, primarily domestically. Also. it will be hard to get the agreement of the European Union countries, especially of those who gained advantageous positions in Romania, some of which are essentially colonial by their nature.

The following measures can be taken even in the current legal system, or at which, we hope, there will be less opposition in the Romanian political class. This way it would be possible, as alternative to the IMF-imposed program, to collect significant funds for the state budget, and so to improve the country's current financial situation. In addition, these money funds could be used to stimulate the national economy (investments, promotion, etc.).

The actions considered are the following:

- - The cancellation of the annual subsidies and of the electoral campaign subsidies granted to political parties. Those who want to do politics should do it with their own money, or drawn from subscriptions and donations;

- - The cancellation of the grants to associations, except those strictly necessary for survival of the Romanian nation. Examples of associations to which the subsidies can canceled are: the associations of the national minorities, the Democratic Union of Hungarians in Romania ('UDMR'), the publishers associations, the cultural unions (they can live by their own creations) and the animal welfare organizations. We are in desperate position to protect human life first, then the animals. It's wrong to spend more to maintain a stray dog than for a retired or disabled person;

- - Drastic reduction of the Parliament expenses (maximum 200 MPs, a limitation of the parliamentary staff per representative to a counselor, a secretary and a driver, abolishing the representatives of the national minorities, lower administrative and representation costs, etc.);

- - The cancellation of the allowances of councilors from the village council up to the municipality and to the county councils. The money saved in this way can be used for local economic investment. In addition, thus would break down the territorial political and economical mafia, making way for competent and honest politicians;

- - Because after December 1989, the politicians at all levels in Romania have enriched themselves continuously and without measure in the periods when they were in power, while the vast majority of the population have impoverished increasingly, is necessary for ministers and those holding elective offices (President, MPs, mayors, members of the commune, town, municipal and county councils, etc.) not to exceed two terms of four years;

- - Reducing the huge salaries and bonuses received by leaders of the National Bank of Romania, of the Ministry of the Finance National, of the Tax Administration National Agency ('ANAF') and of the National Companies, and returning to normal payments in these sectors which believe to be state within a state. This would bring annually tens of millions to the state budget;

- The staffing and the payment schemes of the national radio and television, should be resized. In the spirit of free market, taking money for radio and TV subscription in the electricity bill should be stopped. Also, their subsidies from the state budget should be stopped. Each radio and TV station should live of its own work;

- To make savings by reducing the foreign diplomatic personnel from countries where Romania has no economic interest, by reducing wages over 3,000 euros, by reducing the travel allowances of MPs, by limiting the amount of currency that a tourist may take out of the country, etc.;

- Saving important money funds by the abolition of the National Council for the Study of the Security-police Archives ('CNSAS'). This institution was established following the diversion "Security-police - terrorists" in December 1989 and its scope was abolished by the checks made by the media, by the prosecutors and by the judges. After over 22 years since the dissolution of the Romanian Security-police, is unnecessary to discuss what it did and how it worked;

- The abolition of the Institute for the study of communist crimes, because those crimes and abuses were due to the Soviet occupation regime established after the Second World War in Romania. In this way significant money will be saved;

- - Abolishing the Romanian Cultural Institute and to transfer its budget to the Ministry of Foreign Affairs Ministry, which can fulfill better the tasks of promoting Romanian culture abroad;
- - To apply strict and severe taxes to people who practice retrograde professions, such as astrology, witchcraft, riddles, etc. And also to bioenergy therapists of any kind.;
- - Severe taxation of imports of luxury -yachts, expensive cars of over 20,000 euros, helicopters, jewelry, etc.;
- - Doubling taxes on any commercials: posters, leaflets, advertisements in newspapers, TV clips, etc. Most companies practice an aggressive advertising, so they have enough money to pay these taxes;
- - The substantial increase in taxes on alcoholic beverages because they are more dangerous than cigarettes and are consumed by more people;
- - The cancellation of the masked salary of the clergy of all denominations, as these religious propagandists (priests, Mufti, etc.) are providers of services paid by individuals, not state employees. Currently, the clergy of all denominations are "helped" by the state with incredibly high monthly amounts, for example: the Patriarch of the Romanian Orthodox Church

with 8,300 RON (1,900 euros -compared with the average salary of 325 euros), the religious leaders (Chief Mufti, etc.) with 7,600 RON (1,740 euros), the bishop with 6,600 RON (1,510 euros), the auxiliary bishop with 6,350 RON (1,450 euros), etc. We deal with people who receive free meals, house, transport, clothes etc. and have no family obligations. Why they need this money, when it is plucked from the mouth of the dying poor?!;

- • - The cancellation of all the grants, donations and restitutions made to religious groups in the last 22 years and the money to be repaid to the state budget. The recovered buildings to enter into the national property and to receive economic, humanitarian or modern cultural destinations;
- • - The abolition of the religion teacher jobs, and the money thus obtained to be given to the Ministry of Education, in order to save other science teaching positions strictly necessary to cultivating the young generations (astronomy, natural and exact sciences, etc.). Religion should be taught after American model: voluntarily, in Sunday schools, in family or in churches;
- • - The secularization of the assets of religious cults and sects not used for practicing rituals or being contrary to their basic dogma ("Do not store up for yourselves treasures on earth...") based on the model applied by Prince

Alexandru Ioan Cuza. Currently, the religious cults and sects are richer than the Romanian state, and their wealth of tens of billion euros was accumulated largely from donations, grants and restitution made from the state budget or from the national patrimony. The money thus obtained to be directed to the pension fund and the buildings to be used for humanitarian purposes (orphanages, nursing homes, special schools, etc.);

- - The revenues and wealth of all religious cults should be taxed, as of any other economic company. The religious cults get important incomes from several categories of economic activities: rituals, religious taxes, travel (hostels, hotels, etc.), publishing services, handicrafts, agricultural-industrial activities, "Sanctification" of movable and immovable, trade with religious objects etc. The Greeks, to whom the Christian religion is due, apply a tax of 20% to the religious revenues;

- - The money donated by the Romanian Government and by various ministries for the building of "the cathedral of nation's salvation" and of other places of worship should be repaid. The Romanian Orthodox Church defies this poor nation, by refusing to stop pharaonic constructions and by refusing to help the restoration of the old religious monuments;

- - Ending the masked subsidies for car sales

through buying old cars by the state, in the so-called "RABLA" program;

- - Introducing a fee of 50,000 euros for granting Romanian citizenship. Thus, the citizens from developing countries will not come to Romania, to be maintained from its already anemic budget;
- - Ceasing subsidies for raw materials and energy (gas, electricity, etc..) to all Romanian and foreign companies. It is not normal to subsidize companies producing aluminum, cars and chemical fertilizers and the domestic consumers to pay the electricity twice as expensive than the industrial users;
- - Suspension of imports of weapons and combat equipment for a period of five years, since products in this category are old and do not serve the national defense;
- - The withdrawal of Romanian troops in Afghanistan, as did the most advanced European nations, and the termination of the costs for their maintenance;
- - The revenues from fines should be increased substantially, as many Romanian citizens are disorderly, undisciplined and have uncivilized behavior. Should be enacted or increased the fines for: soiling public environment, public disturbance, use of vulgar expressions in public, breach of civilized behavior on public transport, illegal possession of weapons, walking drunk on

the streets, auto and pedestrian rules violations (speeding, alcohol, illegal parking, passing on the red, etc.), destruction of green areas and of the trees, maltreatment of minors and women, etc.;

- - The Romanians are living a painful paradox; people who worked 30-40 years receive a pension of 7-800 RON (160-182 euros) per month, and for maintaining an offender sentenced to prison it is consumed about 2,500 RON (572 euros) per month. So, forced labor for 10-12 hours a day it is needed to be enacted again. Only then the criminals will feel that they are punished and will pay their own maintenance;

- - In place of imprisonment, for certain offenses, to be introduced the payment of large sums of money. For example, for a negligent injury, instead of three years imprisonment, to be able to pay an amount of 300 RON (68 euros) for each day in prison. The system was applied before and brought great revenues to the state;

- - Most foreign 'investors' have not met the obligations under the privatization contracts. Also, many privatization contracts include clauses that are not in good faith (unfair undervaluation of prices, etc.). According to international practices, all these privatization contracts can be terminated. So, the respective privatizations are voidable. It is necessary that all the fraudulent privatizations or where the obligations were not met to be canceled by

Justice, and those companies should be turned over to the Romanian state. As a first step should be declassified the privatization contracts of 'Petrom', 'Rompetrol', 'Romtelecom', 'Sidex Galati', 'Petrotub Roman', and of the aluminum manufacturing plants, of the distributions of gas, electricity and water, etc.;

- The cancellation of tax exemptions granted by corrupt government officials, in the last 22 years, and the recovery of the amounts due from debtors and from the respective corrupt government officials. On a simple estimate, it is matter at least of 20 billion euros. For example, only 'Rompetrol' and 'Erickson' Companies have been exempted by 800 million dollars each. If corrupt government officials had not applied all those exemptions, today Romania would not have such a high debt abroad;

- The cancellation of the payment rescheduling of taxes payable to the State and emergency collecting of the amounts due from major debtors. Expanding the enforcement on assets held by the present or the former heads of bankrupt companies;

- To take all needed measures to identify and to recover the huge sums of money taken out of the country by the criminals of the Romanian transition;

- Initiation of prosecution, while seizing all assets, of the political-economic and administrative leaders who illegally privatized profitable economic objectives such as 'Petrom', 'Rompetrol', 'Romtelecom', 'BCR' and 'BRD' banks, 'Petrotub', 'IMGB', 'Champagne -Simleul Silvaniei', 'Central Company for Railway Building' ('CCCF'), steel works, gas and electricity distribution networks etc. These companies and many others were profitable, fueled huge amounts of money to the state budget and provided an immense number of jobs, for which their privatization was not justified by economic criteria, but motivated by corruption;

- - Harsh punitive sanctions for economic crimes, as bribery, influence peddling, etc. Application, In all cases of such offenses, the penalty of total or partial confiscation of property has to be applied;
- - For over 22 years, the Romanians are instigated to consumerism, through aggressive and manipulative advertising , so they consume unnecessary and harmful goods and services (pornography, alcohol, astrology, magic, violent and horror movies, that affect them mentally, etc.). A broad process of education against all these goods and services, has to be triggered. The slogan "Buy Romanian goods and services to enhance your situation" has to be promoted. The Romanian citizens must learn to consume less than they produce and to save strictly. It is also imperative to be restored the cult of work and of honesty;

- • - Economic analysts have estimated that the underground economy in Romania is about 10 billion euros per year. It is appropriate, as in the West, that reporting offenses of any kind, including unauthorized work and tax evasion, to be considered a patriotic duty. Subordinated to the National Integrity Agency ("ANI") and organized territorially, to operate honest citizens committees (especially retirees), which will report all cases of unauthorized work, tax evasion, smuggling, etc.;
- • - The re-establishment of the Ministry of Foreign Trade and of the county offices of foreign trade, through which small Romanian entrepreneurs will be able to perform all export activities: information on foreign markets, advertising and promotion on foreign markets, making exports and collecting of the amounts due;
- • - Before December 1989, there were Romanian state companies that have built abroad, refineries, fertilizer plants, cement plants, poultry, high voltage power lines, berths and port dams, roads, bridges, tunnels and dams. Also, they were prospecting and drilling wells for oil and gas. Those companies were required not only in the Middle East and North Africa but also in highly developed foreign countries (FRG, for example). It is necessary to reestablish those state companies, with former and well-qualified specialists and young people trained on their job,

eliminating from the Romanian sites the plundering foreign companies, chosen by corrupt rulers. This will create jobs, reduce unemployment and will result in savings, because the Romanians, in those kind of activities, work cheaper and better;

- - Urgent actions for the judicious management of the national land, from which we mention the followings: banning land sale to foreigners, except to the EU citizens; the legalization of land donations to the state or to the specialized scientific institutions (research stations, agricultural academies, etc.); the confiscation of the wealth of those who, for purposes of speculation, have cleared orchards, vineyards and forests; the re-establishment of state research farms and stations in agriculture and horticulture with the land thus obtained or recovered; prohibition of land donations to religious cults and sects, because they may not have wealth, according to their tenets; replacing the traditional cultures with those more profitable (trees and shrubs, grapes, green vegetables, herbs, flowers, exotic plants. Cereals only on large areas with possibilities of mechanization and irrigation.); the national irrigation system rehabilitation as state property; the reestablishment of the national procurement and export of agricultural and agricultural-industrial products, including organic vegetables, fruit crops and berries, mushrooms etc. Also, to establish a coherent system of peasant markets, aligned along the main road communications;

- - Severe progressive taxation of owners of numerous homes and of the luxury degree as well. In addition to increase the revenues to the budget, this way the speculation with housing will be stopped and they will renounce the oversized and ultra luxurious buildings;

- - Because, in Romania the gasoline and diesel oil prices have increased even when oil barrel price went down, the Office of Competition and the Consumer Protection Office have to take action to seize the proceeds of these speculations;

- - The prices of some basic foodstuffs in Romania are higher than in the West, despite the fact that wages are about 4-8 times smaller. The Office for Consumer Protection has to compel foreign supermarkets and hypermarkets to sell products at prices existing in the West or lower, in line with lower revenues of the Romanians;

- - Legalization and taxation of prostitution, based on the existing model in Western countries; this way in addition to the budget revenues, rape, venereal diseases spread and illicit income for the pimps will be prevented.

C - Conclusions

The rights won by the Romanians in December 1989 (multi-party system, freedom of speech, free elections, etc.) are obviously of paramount importance. At the time of communist dictatorship, not only we did not have this essay published, but we would not have the right to address such issues.

But not less important is that every citizen should have the right not to starve (beeing for example, a long time unemployed without any income). Unacceptable is also the reality in which, the rich countries grab the wealth and natural monopolies of the poor countries; this even in the situation when all these countries are member states of the same European Union.

Some of the planet's resources are being depleted and the pollution has become almost uncontrollable. More and more billions will be added to the current population of the globe. Illusionary is the believe of those who think that, with the advance into civilization, population growth will stagnate. Birth rate is a function not only of the developmnet level of a nation, but also of factors such as religion, traditions etc. Population explosion will not be stopped neither by wars or via the "gunboat diplomacy" (which became today's 'diplomacy of aircraft carriers'). At the present potential of destruction accumulated, a generalized war could lead to the final catastrophe. It is known that the dinosaurs disappeared from the planet earth. So, if the current situation is irresponsibly managed, we could reach the end of human society, as well.

Given these realities, we believe that the inequality reached today between men and between nations as well, can not continue. To paraphrase a statement of a great thinker, we would say that "the twenty first century will be of equality between men and nations, or will not be at all" This matter will be very difficult to accept by the rich and powerful countries, because to achieve such a goal, they will have to slow their economic growth and to support effectively the development of nations lagging behind. There is no other solution!

In their writings ('Capital', 'The Communist Manifesto' etc.), Marx and Engels issued, in the mid-nineteenth century, the theory according to which the communism would represent the final solution for the human society. After October 1917, Lenin and Stalin have started to put into practice the theory of the building of communism, the "golden dream of mankind" as it was called by some. We know, what kind of society was actually built! Then suddenly, between 1989-1991, the Soviet-style communism collapsed like a house of cards. The USSR and the east-european regimes were self-decomposed; especially due to their economic inefficiency and due to the fact that they could not face the arms race which intensified to the end of twentieth century.

Some believe that the true final solution is the "end of history" predicted by Professor Francis Fukuyama. We dare to believe that as long as the mankind will survive, there will be no end of history. Professor Anghel N. Rugina said: "The history of the future is always an open book where the unexpected may play a significant role." The human beings, by their nature, will always crave for something else. Only the human extinction on the Planet Earth, can cause the permanent loss of his desire for change. So, sooner or later the almighty neoliberalism will fall too. Nothing is forever! Only change is eternal!

Quicker will increase the polarization of the world in 'paupers and rich', sooner another socio-economic organization of humanity will occur. The change will be speeded up by the overgrowth of unemployment, by the environmental pollution and by the uncontrolled explosion of world population. We can see that every day is accelerating the exploatation of sources of raw materials and especially of the energy resources. Today, that is done until the resources are exhausted completely. In the meantime, the fights (violent and nonviolent) for these resources intensify. As World War I led to the two Russian revolutions and the Second World War and the Cold War led to the emergence of the Chinese giant, so the extension of current military operations around the world could lead to new major surprises. Unfortunately, nations do not believe in the biblical perception: "All who take the sword will die by the sword" (The New Testament,

Matthew 16: 52). So the future remains open to any eventuality. Absolutely certain is that sociocultural evolution of mankind can not be stopped by anyone!

March 24, 2012

P. S. This essay represents the translation, by its authors, of the text in Romanian language.